THE SECRET
of the
HARVEST

Mobilizing for Team Evangelism

THE SECRET
of the
HARVEST

Mobilizing for Team Evangelism

WARREN L. HOFFMAN

Evangel  301 N. Elm St.
Press Nappanee, Indiana 46550

Cover design: Glen Pierce

Library of Congress Catalog Card Number: 88-81961

ISBN: 0-916035-25-5

PHOTOTYPESET ◖Ⓠ◗ FOR QUALITY

Printed in the United States of America

3 2

To
Ira Eyster
who worked at my side as
we learned to evangelize

Contents

A Word to the Reader

In the earliest days of his public ministry, Jesus saw two brothers fishing from the shore of Lake Galilee. "Come, follow me," Jesus said, "and I will make you fishers of men."

Do you notice that Jesus invited both brothers to become fishers of men? He called Peter, the persuasive, articulate, older brother. He also called Andrew, the quiet, friendly, younger brother. No, Andrew was not just standing nearby as Jesus spoke to Peter. Jesus promised *both* brothers, "I will make you fishers of men."

We can infer from Jesus' words that neither brother was ready for evangelism at that time. Translated literally from the Greek, his words are: "I will make you *become* fishers of men." The implied promise is that Jesus would teach each brother how to use his particular strengths and temperament effectively in the work of evangelism.

As we read the Gospels and Acts, that is exactly what happened. After being trained by Jesus, Peter became an effective public speaker. He persuasively proclaimed the good news about Jesus to *crowds* of people. On the day of Pentecost it was Peter who stepped forward to speak to the large crowd that had gathered (Acts 2:14-40). Before long, he was preaching to more crowds (Acts 3:11-26). When he was arrested, he spoke to an assembly of national leaders (Acts 4:1-22). He traveled to outlying areas, and then to other countries, to talk to groups of people wherever they gathered (Acts 8:14-25; 9:32-43; 10:1-48).

In contrast to his "stage front" brother, Andrew was quiet and unassuming. But he had a knack for warm, friendly conversation. As he was being trained, Andrew shared the good news with *individual persons*. He talked first with his older brother Peter and brought him to Jesus (John 1:40-42). Another time he talked to a boy with some loaves and fishes and brought him to Jesus (John 6:8-9). When others hesitated, he talked with some Greeks and brought them to Jesus, prompting Jesus to announce that the good news is for everyone (John 12:20-22, 32). Andrew's approach was quiet and unobtrusive. Yet one by one he brought people to Jesus.

True to his word, Jesus made *both* brothers "fishers of men." Both brothers were eminently successful, each in his own way, because Jesus taught each brother to use his unique gifts and temperament effectively in the work of evangelism.

Jesus will do the same for us! Whatever our aptitudes, personality, and experiences, there is a crucial place for us in evangelism. Jesus' promise, "I will make you fishers of men," is for each of us. As we listen and learn from him, he will teach us to "fish" just as he taught Andrew and Simon Peter.

In this book you will discover opportunities in evangelism that "fit" you. Whether you consider yourself to be a "natural" in evangelism like Peter or an "unlikely" evangelist like Andrew, there is a way for you to contribute to the work of evangelism. I am so certain of this that I will promise: if you have a will to work in evangelism, this book will show you a way.

I am able to make such a brash promise because evangelism is a much broader—and varied—task than *telling* the good news. Many of us visualize evangelism as public speaking in a revival or crusade. Or we may think of it as presenting the gospel to another individual in a personal conversation. Either way, the work of evangelism is construed, essentially, as announcing the good news. If we have done little public speaking or are uncomfortable confronting individual persons, we may conclude that evangelism is not for us.

In recent years this narrow conception of evangelism has been challenged by proponents of the church growth movement. It is not enough to *tell* the good news, they are saying. The task of evangelism is to *make disciples*.

In this way of thinking, evangelism is not complete until disciples are made and the results are evident in their lives. C. Peter Wagner articulates this inclusive description of evangelism as "all that is involved in bringing men and women who do not have a personal relationship with Jesus Christ into fellowship with him and into responsible church membership."[1]

Understood in this way, evangelism begins with the earliest contact with an unsaved person. It includes the kind of friendship and helpfulness that creates interest in the gospel. It moves to the communication of the good news. It continues with formative teaching in the Christian faith and life. And it culminates in the incorporation of a committed new disciple into the fellowship of the church as a contributing member.

To accomplish the total task of making disciples, a multitude of gifts and aptitudes are needed. Just as important as the gift of telling the good news are gifts of intercession, encouragement, and teaching. Also vital, as we shall see, are gifts of leadership, miracles, healing, hospitality, helps, and service.

Since no one of us is equally proficient in all of these gifts, this kind of evangelism requires a team of persons working together. One person with the gift of proclamation may be able to produce a convert. But no one, working alone, can make a disciple. The task of making disciples requires a full complement of gifts, which is only available when persons work cooperatively.

This means that *your* gifts and aptitudes, whatever they are, are needed for evangelism. The contribution you can make is essential for a complete "mix" of gifts. As you participate in a cooperative effort, *you* can effectively contribute to the work of evangelism. *You* can help to win persons to Christ and his Church in your community!

This book is an invitation for you to get in on the action. The book presents the basic biblical principles that undergird evangelism. It explains *how* you can participate in the work of evangelism. And it suggests ways to work together to effectively evangelize. The aim throughout is to inform and motivate, so that you can take action—with a team—to evangelize the unchurched persons in your community.

Think of this book as a tool box, a sort of "starter kit." As you grasp the concepts that are presented and practice the skills that are suggested, you will be equipped for your first initiatives in evangelism.

If you are reading this book by yourself, find a partner and practice the skills together. Better yet, study these concepts and practice these skills with a group of interested persons as a potential evangelistic team—in the context of a Sunday school class, youth group, or church.

If you will act on what you learn, you will be launched into a challenging and rewarding enterprise. You will develop the skills of "fishing" for men and women, boys and girls, and experience the thrills of seeing them entrust their lives to the living Christ. I hope that will be enough to whet your appetite for a lifetime of active evangelism!

A Word to Teachers, Leaders, and Pastors

The aim of this book is to inform and motivate persons to take action—with a team—to evangelize unchurched persons in your community. Whatever your past experience in evangelism, you can aspire to this high aim!

First, you need to determine how this study can serve your congregation best. In conversation with the leadership of your church, assess where your church, group, or class *is* in evangelistic effectiveness. Then agree on what you will aspire to *become*.

- Have you been "spinning your wheels" in evangelism, not knowing how to begin? This book can serve you as a "starter kit" to equip you for your first initiatives in evangelism. Plan to study these concepts and practice these skills as a potential evangelistic team—in a church-wide initiative, or in a youth group or Sunday school class.

- Has your evangelism proceeded in "fits and starts" as you attempt one approach and then another, only to see each of your initiatives falter for one reason or another? This book can enable you to "fill in the gaps" in your efforts. It presents a comprehensive "package" of biblical principles and evangelistic skills which, when all have been laid in place, can enable you to resuscitate a faltering—or failed—evangelistic initiative.

- Are you already active in evangelism and experiencing good results? This book can serve you as an initial training course for new persons as they begin to work with you in evangelism.

Second, plan a time for the study group to practice evange-listic skills. Locate a two-hour block of prime time for an evangelistic team to meet weekly. In the first hour, team members can gather for instruction and training. In the second, they can scatter for the evangelistic work of prayer, witness, encouragement, and teaching.

If you are studying the book for an hour each week in a Sunday school class or youth group, plan for an additional hour each week to do the activities suggested at the end of each chapter. If this is not possible, extend your study to 26 weeks rather than 13, and alternate between biblical concepts one week and practical assignments the next. If you want your group to help make the decision about a time to practice evangelistic skills (as suggested in Activity 3 of Chapter 1), be prepared to suggest several workable possibilities.

Throughout the course of your study, keep the leadership of your congregation informed about the skills you are learning and the community contacts you are actually making. (This is especially crucial if the pastor is not leading the study or a member of the study group.)

Please do *not* use this book with a group or a class that has no intention of practicing the skills. Few of us need to expand our knowledge of evangelism. We already know far more than we are able to do. Our aim is to provide a way for any person to participate in evangelism. If your group is not ready to *apply* the biblical principles in actual evangelistic experiences, it would be better to postpone the study.

Third, determine to lead your group as a teacher/trainer— one who will both *teach* and *demonstrate* the principles of evangelism. As a teacher/trainer, you will be teaching biblical concepts and inviting the group to follow your example as you apply and practice the basic skills of evangelism.

If you feel that you are unable to do this because of your inexperience in evangelism, try reading through the entire book. As you read, the Holy Spirit can assure you that what first may look like the "overwhelming" task of evangelism can be broken down into "bite-size" skills which *you* can manage, even without prior evangelistic experience. In addition, commit up to one hour a day to practice evangelism. You may want to ask someone who is experienced in evangelism to assist you as a mentor.

The best teacher/trainer is not necessarily an expert in

evangelism, but is one who is actively learning and practicing the basic skills. Even if you are only two or three weeks ahead of your group, you can teach what you are learning—with fresh, vivid, firsthand accounts of your initial experiences. On the weeks when you are definitely "in over your head," ask your mentor to serve the group as teacher/trainer for that session.

If you still feel you are unable to serve the group as a teacher/trainer, step aside for someone else who can. Join the class as a learner and, under the direction of an experienced trainer, prepare to give active leadership in evangelism once the training is completed. (In this regard, review Worksheet 15, p. 235, which outlines responsibilities of a team leader when evangelistic outreach actually begins.)

Fourth, be sure to prepare at least *two or three weeks ahead* for each group session. Before the study begins, read through the entire book, including the worksheets, paying special attention to Chapters 1 and 9. Become familiar with the biblical concepts. Look at the activities at the end of each session. Some can be done in class as a group. But most are actual evangelizing experiences, and will require you to work ahead of time to make the necessary arrangements. Note the suggestions on p. 199 for ways to use the worksheets.

For example, gather the statistics you will need for the *first session*. Decide on a time—or work out several possible times— to practice the evangelistic skills discussed in Chapter 1.

In advance of *session two*, begin praying the evangelistic prayers. Gather copies of the church or class directory for each participant.

For *session three*, develop a list of unchurched persons who are prospective participants in your church. Explore ways to identify newcomers in your community. Using Worksheet 4, practice contacting newcomers by telephone. Select a nearby neighborhood and try approaching persons door-to-door with the survey in Worksheet 6.

As you can, set up appointments to visit in preparation for *session four*. Develop your own personal testimony. If you have scheduled any appointments to visit, select one or two other persons and practice your visitation skills in advance.

Continue to prepare in this way several weeks in advance of each session.

Finally, if your congregation does not have a planned approach to evangelism, lay the groundwork throughout the study for an ongoing evangelistic initiative. Communicate the vision of an evangelistic team which will meet regularly each week. Emphasize the diversity of abilities which contribute to the work of evangelism. Share your conviction that an earnest band of aspiring evangelists—however small—can have an infectious impact on your entire church.

As enthusiasm for evangelism mounts, work with the leadership of your church to design an evangelistic initiative that fits your congregation and community. Following the steps in Chapter 9, "Making It Happen," establish an ongoing opportunity for persons to participate in evangelism. As you do this, you and your group will be launching into a challenging and rewarding enterprise—the adventure of evangelism!

Acknowledgements

The good news that each of us can participate in the work of evangelism has been an exciting personal discovery. Though I have never considered myself an evangelist, I accepted an assignment as a church planting pastor. I soon discovered that new churches are not started without evangelism! So I plunged into the adventure of learning to "fish" for men and women, boys and girls.

My wife Connie and our daughters have been active partners in this venture of risk and learning. In addition, the Lord brought to our side three choice couples to help us in our earliest attempts: Ira and Ernestine Eyster, Gene and Mary Blessing, and Ed and Marj Strayer.

In the past years the Spirit has raised up an evangelistic team in our congregation, and this book is most directly the results of the insights and practices I shared and refined with them: Stan and Carolyn Engle, Chuck and Carol Freels, Ava Linden, Caryle Lulla, Linda Munson and daughter Jodie, Pat Parker, Carla Richerson, April Rhodes, Rich and Jackie Sevetsky, with their daughters Lynn and Chrissy, Jim and Jerry Stetler, Ed and Marj Strayer and their children Drew and Sarah, Diane Watts, Leslie and Julie Wegele, and, from my own family, Connie, Erin, Brooke, Carrie, and Laurel.

The impetus for writing came from the Brethren in Christ Church through its Commission on Christian Education Literature. Ed Strayer took on extra responsibilities as a summer assistant pastor to allow me time for writing. Sandy Everett has done all the typing. A nearby pastor, Arly Johnson, gave valuable suggestions on writing style. Don Shafer, John Hawbaker, and

Dale Shaw offered a broad range of counsel as an editorial committee. Glen Pierce, my editor, and his assistant, Helen Johns, ably guided the book from inception to completion.

In the fullest sense this book is *our* story. The intention throughout is to present enduring biblical principles which are applicable anywhere and to anyone. But our discovery of them is an inescapable part of their presentation. As a result, the book contains numerous incidents from our experience here in Oklahoma City. To spare any of these people embarrassment, I have generally altered names in relating these experiences. But let me assure you, none of the incidents are fictional. Nor are any of them composites of the experiences of several individuals. All are actual experiences in our venture of learning to evangelize.

We are living illustrations of Jesus' readiness to fulfill his promise: "I will make you fishers of men." In the confidence that he will do the same for you, here now is what Jesus has taught us about evangelism.

Warren Hoffman
Oklahoma City, Oklahoma

1

The Secret of the Harvest

In 1980 Connie and I, with our daughters, began a great adventure. We came to Oklahoma City to establish a new church—from scratch! It was the last thing we ever expected to do. As we assessed our aptitudes at the time, we felt that we had gifts in music, communication, innovation, and leadership. But we did not, and still do not, claim the gift of evangelistic preaching. Yet the Spirit was unmistakably directing us to Oklahoma City, and we came.

I began working enthusiastically in all the ways in which I was experienced and comfortable. Before anything else, I spent a full week in prayer. Then I developed a bold and innovative plan. Next, I contacted persons who had been referred to us as potential participants. I invited them to join us in Bible studies. In the hope that they would become the nucleus of the new church, I invested myself in teaching, encouraging, and counseling the ones who responded. I did everything . . . but evangelize.

In time we had a group of appreciative individuals who enjoyed the teaching and fellowship we were providing. Our prayers, plans, Bible studies, and activities were all helpful to them. But only a few of these persons were willing to commit themselves to one another as a new congregation. After two years of hard work, we had not established a church. We were failing.

More than anything else, it was the sobering prospect of imminent failure that mobilized me to evangelize. That will not go down in the annals of my personal history as a glorious moment. And I am not recommending this particular motivation. But when I squarely faced the choice to evangelize or to fail, I chose to evangelize. I swallowed hard and plunged in. My motivation, as I have indicated, was deplorable. My training in the area of evangelism was negligible. My initial attempts can only be characterized as inept. The only thing I had going for me at that point was that I had taken the plunge. I had begun the work of evangelism.

At the time I didn't realize how decisive that step was. But with several years of reflection since then, I have concluded that the most important thing that any of us can do in evangelism is simply to begin. To lay aside misconceptions, to step out in spite of fears, to proceed even with mixed motivations, to disregard any perceived lack of aptitude, to throw all reservations to the wind, and just begin: these are the decisive first steps in evangelism.

This insight, like all of the others we have come to, is rooted in the Bible. In Matthew 9:35-38 we discover the "secret" of reaching the unchurched persons in our communities and, ultimately, throughout the world for Jesus Christ. It is the readiness of each of us to participate in the work of evangelism.

Jesus went through all the towns and villages, teaching in their synagogues, preaching the good news of the kingdom and healing every disease and sickness. When he saw the crowds, he had compassion on them, because they were harassed and helpless, like sheep without a shepherd. Then he said to his disciples, "The harvest is plentiful but the workers are few. Ask the Lord of the harvest, therefore, to send out workers into his harvest field."

Earlier, Matthew had reported Jesus' first tour through the cities and villages of Galilee (Matt. 4:23). Here he summarizes the impact of a second tour. Twice now, people throughout Galilee had heard the stirring announcement, "Repent, for the kingdom of heaven is near" (Matt. 4:17). Everywhere, they had been amazed at teaching like that found in the Sermon on the Mount (Matt. 5, 6, 7). Many had been healed of chronic and terminal illnesses (Matt. 8 and 9). As we might expect, this teaching and healing had stirred an overwhelming response. Large crowds, sometimes numbering into the thousands, gathered to see and hear Jesus (Matt. 14:13-21; 15:29-38).

Vast numbers, great need

As Jesus looked into the sea of faces, he perceived that these vast numbers of people were "harassed" and "helpless." With the word translated "harassed" Jesus pictured people, like sheep, who had been harried and plundered by predators. Originally meaning flayed or mangled, this word had come to mean vexed, annoyed, and utterly wearied. Now the people were helpless, like sheep who had been upended and were unable to regain their footing.

Even after two full mission tours, Jesus was inundated by human need.

And so are we.

Almost one million persons live in the six contiguous counties that comprise the Greater Oklahoma City area. Even though Oklahoma has been characterized as part of the "Bible belt," only half of these persons have any church affiliation according to current statistics. By our own observation and informal surveys, even fewer are in church on any given Sunday. That means that at least 500,000 persons in the Greater Oklahoma City area are unchurched and most likely unsaved. In the crowds around us here there are half a million "harassed" and "helpless" people!

Not long ago I was preparing to speak at a church in Pennsylvania, and gathered similar statistics for the local community. I discovered that in the county, only 56 percent of the people were affiliated with any church. (That is higher than many areas of the country, to be sure.) The population of the town, I learned from the Chamber of Commerce, is 8,900 persons. When I applied the percentage of unchurched persons in the county to this commmunity, I calculated that, out of almost 9,000 persons, nearly 4,000 are unchurched. And that's just within the borough limits.

When I expanded that population figure to include the surrounding townships—the area that comprises the local school district—the figure rises to 18,000 persons, with 8,000 of them unchurched. The congregation which invited me to speak has a normal worship attendance of 350, and could easily be satisfied, except that it is located in the midst of a potential harvest field of 8,000 unchurched persons!

If you were to develop statistics for your community, they

would be similar. *All* of us are surrounded by crowds of people who are hurting in the very same ways as the crowds surrounding Jesus. In the rough and tumble of life, the people have been flayed, mangled, and plundered. They are weary and utterly helpless.

Varying motivations

How do we respond to such overwhelming need?

Jesus' response, Matthew reports, was one of compassion. The word Matthew uses here is the strongest word available in the Greek language. It describes a convulsive pity which moves a person to the depths of his or her being.

From the other instances when this word for compassion is used to describe Jesus' response, we can identify the kinds of needs that moved Jesus so deeply—demonization (Mark 9:22), sickness (Matt. 14:14), hunger (Matt. 15:32), blindness (Matt. 20:34), the loneliness caused by disease (Mark 1:41) and the pain of death (Luke 7:13). No doubt these deep and varied hurts were prevalent in the crowds surrounding Jesus.

Like Jesus, we may be motivated by compassion when we encounter persons with needs like these. Consider the story of Dora, who began to attend our worship services as often as she could within the constraints of her husband Larry's full schedule of weekend recreation. Shortly after, she was personally renewed through the Holy Spirit. Since then her faith has been growing and her continuing hope is that Larry will respond to the good news and accept Christ as Savior and Lord. Larry is easy to like. He is straight-talking and helpful. He has heart problems and, in a sense, is living on borrowed time. For all of these reasons and more, Dora is motivated by compassion to pray and work for Larry's salvation.

Others, seeing the same crowds, may be motivated by conviction. John, one of Jesus' apostles wrote: "That which was from the beginning, which we have heard, which we have seen with our eyes, which we have looked at and our hands have touched—this we proclaim concerning the Word of life" (1 John 1:1). Jesus Christ had so profoundly impacted the lives of the apostles that they could not keep the good news for only themselves. Their own personal experience of Jesus' love and power and wisdom was completely satisfying, and they were utterly convinced that Jesus would do the same for everyone. They were motivated to tell the good news out of deep personal conviction.

In our congregation we often begin our worship services with Scripture choruses, accompanied by guitars. When we sing "I Have Decided to Follow Jesus," one of the women in our congregation often sings with tears running down her cheeks. They are the tears of conviction. She knows the impact that Jesus Christ has had on her life, transforming her from an alcoholic who had lost all hope to a devoted wife and mother. She prays for her children and encourages them to come to church. She participates eagerly in the witness and service of our church. She knows that what Jesus Christ has done for her, he will do for others. She is motivated by conviction.

Still others may be motivated by the command of Jesus. In Matthew 28:19-20, Jesus commissions every believer to make disciples: "Therefore go and make disciples of all nations, baptizing them in the name of the Father and of the Son and of the Holy Spirit, and teaching them to obey everything I have commanded you."

This command to make disciples is repeated five times in the New Testament—in Matthew, Mark, Luke, John, and Acts.* And it is just that—a command. It is not a suggestion. It is not an option. It is not assigned to some, and not to others. It is a command charging *all* of us to participate in the work of making disciples.

One of our men, Ira, may have had other motivations when he began going door-to-door with me five years ago, but one of them was certainly obedience to the command of Jesus. To accompany me, he traveled 68 miles (round trip) from his home. Many weeks he would travel the same distance on a second evening and again on Saturday. In that effort we contacted over 500 homes in an approach that was new to us, scary, not innately motivating, and short on any immediate reward. We did not know the people and, in such a brief contact at the door, could hardly discern any sense of personal need, so compassion did not motivate us. Growing up in a Christian home and having

---

*Matt. 28:19-20; Mark 16:15; Luke 24:46-49; John 20:21-23; Acts 1:8.

accepted the Lord at an early age, Ira did not have the acute conviction of a radically transformed life. In the place of these, he was motivated by the command of Jesus. It is a directive that transcends background, emotions, aptitude, preparation, and impacts *all* of us. If nothing else moves us, we must respond to the command of our Lord, Jesus Christ.

Frankly, the Lord Jesus will use *any* motivation for work in his harvest field. If we are short on compassion, weak on conviction, unmoved by his command, *anything* will do. In Philippians 1:15-18, the Apostle Paul wrote from prison: "Some preach Christ out of envy and rivalry, but others out of good will. The latter do so in love, knowing that I am put here for the defense of the gospel. The former preach Christ out of selfish ambition, not sincerely, supposing that they can stir up trouble for me while I am in chains. But what does it matter? The important thing is that in every way, whether from false motives or true, Christ is preached. And because of this I rejoice." When Jesus Christ is proclaimed, regardless of the motivation, the Spirit of God will work. Persons are drawn to Christ and lives are changed forever.

I can attest to this in my life. My motivations were woefully mixed as we came to Oklahoma City. One of my motivations was simply to have an opportunity to give primary pastoral leadership after serving in several associate positions. Another was to have the chance to experiment with various innovations in ministry. One initial motivation was to succeed so impressively that I would make a name for myself. I hope that the motivations of compassion, conviction, and command were at least present in the mix. But I must confess that, if they were, the amount was negligible. These were replaced by an even stronger motivation— my unwillingness to be embarrassed by failure. In Paul's sharp words, I was preaching Christ out of "envy and rivalry" with a strong dose of "selfish ambition."

Yet the miracle is that persons have come to Christ and lives have been changed by the impact of the good news I shared in spite of these deplorable initial motivations. All the while the Spirit has been exposing my motivations and burning away the impurities, I have been fully engaged in the work of evangelism. I do not encourage such impoverished motivations. But I can share from personal experience that any motivation, even some of the poorest ones, are sufficient to begin the work of evangelism.

Common approaches

Once motivated, we face an immediate dilemma because of the vast numbers of people. How do we approach such an overwhelming task?

We might give up. Faced with overwhelming need of any kind, we can be immobilized by the apparent hopelessness of the task. This is certainly true of evangelism. We might think: there are so many unsaved and unchurched persons. What can I do? What difference will my involvement make? I will hardly make a dent in the need! Like Jesus, we may be filled with compassion. But, unlike Jesus, we may react in despair. We might throw up our hands and abandon any attempt at ministering to others.

I can personally attest to the appeal of this option. I would not want to admit how often I've thought about quitting. That I never did is no credit to myself. I really have few marketable skills. I've pumped gas, worked at a feed mill, washed dishes at a restaurant, and taught at seminary. But none of these is a realistic option in Oklahoma City. Since no other opportunities came from anywhere else, I stuck it out. Today we have a healthy, growing church if for no other reason than I didn't give up in despair.

Another typical response is to *alter our approach.* In this technological age, we tend to measure the effectiveness of our methods by the results. When the apparent results are less than we expect, we question our methods. Even worse, we may slip into criticism of a leader who is not—as we view the tasks—getting the job done. Often we conclude that with a change in methodology or leadership, progress would be made. Certainly, this is justified at times. The fact that Jesus could not minister to each individual in the crowds of people surrounding him did not move him to agonized introspection or frantic change. He did not alter his basic approach of teaching, preaching, and healing.

The first method of evangelism I learned here in Oklahoma City was a simple, "no frills" approach to presenting the gospel. I learned a couple of questions to use in starting a conversation, a

basic five-point outline, some key verses, several illustrations—
and was graduated from the seminar.

Not long afterward, I was seated with two other men from
our church in the living room of a young couple. After we became
acquainted, I took a deep (inward) breath, and asked the questions. When I discovered that neither Jerry nor Rachel were
certain of their salvation, I went on with a simple presentation of
the gospel just as I had learned it at the seminar. I concluded as I
had been taught, "Would you like to receive the gift of eternal
life?" To our amazement Jerry and Rachel said yes.

We prayed together and then left without seeing any obvious
evidences of conversion. Jerry and Rachel began attending
church, but before we could provide any appreciable teaching
and nurture, they moved to another city. We wondered how their
newfound faith was faring. Then we received a Christmas card
from them with a personal note—and exciting news. They had
found a church and were now active in its life as teachers of a
Sunday school class.

The seed we had planted was taking root and growing!

Since that time, I have modified that original presentation. I
have changed several illustrations and increased the emphasis on
repentance. Now the tone and content of the presentation
expresses my understanding of the gospel more precisely. But
even in my earliest presentations, when my words were borrowed
and halting, the good news came through. The basic approach
was right.

A third common response is to *work harder*. If some of us
were in Jesus' circumstances here, our knee-jerk response would
be to schedule more evangelistic tours, step up our pace, and put
in longer days in a frantic, misguided effort to reach more people.
But Jesus did not succumb to that temptation. He promised rest
to his disciples (Matt. 11:28-30). And he modeled a diligent,
measured pace.

When we were first learning how to reach unchurched people here in Oklahoma City, a couple of us worked together and
doubled our attendance! The next year, without any help, I
determined to increase by that same amount. I telephoned, wrote
letters and visited. Again, I succeeded. The following winter I
went at it once more with another burst of energy. I lasted three

months until I crashed physically, emotionally, and spiritually. I had pushed myself beyond my limit and fell flat. The doctor called it stress exhaustion. It took five months before I recovered to the point that people began to say, "Warren, you look like your old self again." That was a hard way to learn. But I know now that we don't win the crowds by working ourselves to exhaustion.

The "secret" of the harvest

Jesus rejected all these typical responses. He understood far more clearly than we do the secret of reaching the maximum number of people. It is not despair. It is not better methods. It is not longer days. The secret is to enlist more workers. "Ask the Lord of the harvest, therefore, to send out workers into his harvest field" (Matt. 9:38).

Jesus adopts this plan of action, he explains, because "the harvest is plentiful" (v. 37). There are thousands of people all around us with deep, unmet needs. Among them, people *are* ready—even desperate—to hear the good news about Jesus Christ. A rebellious son or daughter, the person next door, or a callous co-worker may *not* be ready for conversion. But the personal pain of many others is so near the surface that, in Jesus' agricultural analogy, they are ripe for the harvest. They will respond to a clear, loving presentation of the good news.

The only thing needed to "harvest" these hundreds and thousands of hurting persons, Jesus announces, is the mobilization of the maximum number of workers. By mobilizing the maximum number of workers, we will be able to contact the maximum number of persons. And among them we will find the ones whom the Spirit has prepared, the ones who are "ripe" and ready. The size of the harvest is directly proportional to the number of workers. The more workers, the greater the harvest.

Such a realization motivated Jesus to take a decisive step in the expansion of his own ministry: mobilizing more workers. As we follow the pattern Jesus suggests here, we begin by praying, "Lord, send out workers into your harvest field." Then, we step forward to accept our own assignment in the work of reaching people. And no matter who we are, or what we are like, there are important and vital ways that each of us can participate in the work of evangelism.

In our own congregation we have set a goal of "total mobilization," seeking to have our entire membership involved in evangelistic outreach. Since we have the normal diversity of gifts and background, we have to be creative in utilizing a broad range of gifts and aptitudes in our evangelistic efforts.

A number of our people concentrate on prayer. Some give encouragement to persons who are not yet assimilated into the full life of our church. Other persons work behind the scenes to contact people by telephone, asking whether a team of visitors may visit them in their home. Teams of two or three talk with persons in their homes to establish an acquaintance, give a witness, and present the gospel.

As persons accept Christ as Savior, others provide basic teaching in the Christian faith and life—one-to-one—in the home of these new believers. Still other persons care for children to "release" others to serve directly in evangelism. Finally, someone gives overall leadership to an evangelistic team, fitting people and tasks together in a smoothly running operation.

So there *is* a way for each of us to participate in the work of evangelism. All that is required is our willingness to help, in whatever ways we can, to reach persons for Jesus Christ and his church.

This great truth is readily apparent to anyone who lives in the Great Plains of North America and experiences firsthand the annual wheat harvest. With millions of acres under cultivation, equipment engineered with the latest technologies, and the vast distances from Texas to Saskatchewan, an individual worker would be overwhelmed and immobilized.

But thousands of workers are not.

When the wheat ripens in Texas in May, custom harvesters with a bevy of combines, trucks, and other equipment converge on the harvest in Texas. From then on through the summer they slowly move north with the harvest. By the middle of June they are in Oklahoma. In early July they are in Kansas. By early fall, still moving northward, they are harvesting the ripening harvest in Wyoming, Montana, Saskatchewan, and Alberta.

A typical crew may be composed of seven or eight workers, all with complementary skills. Several will operate the gleaners. Others will drive trucks. At least one will be a mechanic. Another will cook. One will be responsible for customer relations. And one will direct the crew as a boss.

Working together, a crew of this size can harvest two to three hundred acres of wheat in a day. Through the course of the summer, the crew might harvest 12,000 acres of wheat. With 3,000 custom harvesting crews operating in the Great Plains each summer, Midwestern farmers are able to harvest a staggering amount of wheat.[2]

Yet no one person has contributed more than a small share of the experience, expertise, and energy. This great harvest enterprise is the cumulative result of thousands of individual workers, cooperating in small crews, with each one making a modest, manageable contribution.

In the same way, Jesus invites each of us to participate in the greatest of all harvests. We cannot delegate the work to specialists and work them to exhaustion. We cannot wait for new, improved methods which will make the work easier. We cannot excuse ourselves on the basis of unsatisfactory motivations. We cannot step aside in feigned humility, protesting that we do not have an evangelistic gift. We cannot claim that our community is already saturated with the gospel. We cannot shrink back from presumed unreceptivity. The Lord of the harvest has cared for each of the contingencies.

The only requirement is the courage to pray, "Lord, send out workers into your harvest" with a readiness to become a full participant in the Lord's answer.

Activities

1. We may be motivated to participate in the work of evangelism by compassion, conviction, command, or for a variety of other reasons. Matthew presents Jesus' motivation as compassion. How would you characterize the primary motivation of Paul? Peter? Andrew? How would you describe your own motivation?

2. A common misconception is that our communities are already saturated with the gospel. Yet Jesus declares that there are crowds of harassed and helpless people all around us. Is this true in your community? Use Worksheet 1 (p. 200) to calculate the number of unchurched persons near you.

3. Few of us need to expand our knowledge of evangelism. We already know far more than we manage to do. We need to be motivated and mobilized to *do* the work of evangelism. The best way to learn the principles and skills introduced in this book is with actual practice. As you begin your study, decide on a time to practice the activities suggested at the end of each chapter.

If you are reading the book with a friend, agree on a time each week when you can meet together to put into action what you are learning. If you are studying the book in a class or group, plan for an additional hour each week to do the activities. If this is not possible, extend your study to 26 weeks, rather than 13, and alternate between biblical concepts one week and practical assignments the next. If you are working with a potential evangelistic team, plan to meet for a two-hour block of time each week. Use the first hour for teaching/learning and the second for doing the work of evangelism.

4. If you are a new trainee with a functioning evangelistic team, accompany trained workers in their work of prayer, witness, encouragement, or teaching as an observer.

2

With Hands Lifted Up

"If you have the will, I'll find a way!" With that brash promise I invited everyone in our congregation to participate in the work of evangelism. Within fifteen minutes Stu and Catherine volunteered. And I was confronted with my first challenge.

This couple lived thirty-five miles away, a fifty-minute drive in both directions. Stu was taking medication for epilepsy and one of the side effects, at times, was confusion and disorientation. In the context of an accepting and supportive church fellowship, Stu and Catherine interacted easily. But it was stressful for Catherine to make new acquaintances. Because they had participated fully in church life through their entire lifetimes, they had had limited exposure with unchurched persons. In addition, they were so familiar with the Bible that their conversation was sprinkled with "church" words and phrases. In the milieu of city life, where people are enamored of appearance and impressions, Stu and Catherine might cause prospective persons to be "put off" rather than attracted.

Yet as they stood before me, I did not question their devotion to the Lord, their eagerness to serve him, or their consistent, faithful Christian lives.

Shaken, but still convinced that everyone can participate in the work of evangelism, I responded, "Thank you, Stu and Catherine. There *is* a way for you to help. Let me pray and think about the possibilities. I'll get back to you."

That week I mulled over possibilities for each of the persons who had volunteered. As I prayed about Stu and Catherine, I recalled a study we had done a number of months earlier on spiritual gifts. At that time Stu and Catherine completed a spiritual gifts profile and scored highest on a particular spiritual gift. This gift requires the vibrant spirituality and deep fervor which Stu and Catherine have. Appearances and first impressions are not essential; earnest sincerity and plainspokenness are far preferable. Broad experience and background are not necessary; singlemindedness is much more valuable. It is not necessary to "meet people" easily or well. While it may be one of the most demanding tasks of all that contribute to the work of evangelism, it is not stressful; in fact, it relieves stress. In this work, distance is not a limiting factor. Stu and Catherine could make this contribution anywhere, anytime. A physical disability, like epilepsy, does not detract. Their church background is not a liability for this task, but a strong and helpful asset.

As I reflected on Stu and Catherine's background and abilities, I knew they were just right for a crucial contribution to our new evangelistic initiative. To both of them, the Lord has given the gift of intercession.

Like Stu and Catherine, your God-given contribution to the work of evangelism may be in prayer. As in every other aspect of the Christian life, prayer is an indispensable prerequisite for effective evangelism.

The necessity of prayer in evangelism

One of the most vivid demonstrations of the necessity of intercessory prayer is reported in Exodus 17. Here the Israelites defeated the Amalekites as Joshua fought and Moses prayed.

Until this time God had fought for the Israelites. In a decisive act of his sovereign power, God had invoked each of the plagues which preceded the Israelites' flight from Egypt. When the Israelites were trapped between the Red Sea and the pursuing Egyptian army, the Lord destroyed the Egyptians. When the Israelites ran out of water, the Lord provided water. When their supply of food was depleted, the Lord provided manna. At each crisis along the way in the exodus from Egypt, God intervened without any human participation except symbolic gestures.

But now for the first time Israel participated *with* God in his work. In response to a fierce, unprovoked attack by marauding Amalekites, Moses directed Joshua to choose some men and go out and *fight*—a human endeavor which would directly impact the outcome of the battle (17:9). Moses, by contrast, assigned to himself a different task. "I will stand on top of the hill with the staff of God in my hands" (17:9). What was Moses doing on the hill? As we retrace some of his actions up to this time, the significance of Moses' staff and upraised hands becomes clear.

At the burning bush God told Moses to throw his staff to the ground. Moses threw down the staff and it became a snake. At God's instruction Moses picked it up and it became an ordinary shepherd's tool once again (Ex. 4:4-5). In his first encounter with Pharaoh, Moses repeated this dramatic transformation. At God's instruction Moses struck the Nile River with his staff to start the plague of water turned to blood (Ex. 7:14-20). Moses stretched out his staff and the plague of hail began (Ex. 9:23). He stretched it out again and Egypt was inundated with locusts (Ex. 10:13). When he stretched out his staff over the Red Sea, the water divided so that the Israelites could cross (Ex. 14:16). When the water supplies were depleted, Moses struck the rock at Rephidim with his staff, and water poured out (Ex. 17:1-7). By this time this staff was no longer identified as a shepherd's staff. It had become "the staff of God." (Ex. 17:9). For Moses and all of the Israelites, it was a symbol of the power of God.

The biblical account refers to Moses' hands less often, but just as meaningfully. "Then Pharaoh . . . said to them, 'Pray to the Lord, for we have had enough thunder and hail. . . .' Moses replied, 'When I have gone out of the city, I will spread my hands in prayer to the Lord. . . .' " Moses left Pharaoh and went out of the city. Then "he spread his hands toward the Lord; thunder and hail stopped, and the rain no longer poured down on the land" (Ex. 9:28-33). Here Moses clearly used his hands in a gesture of prayer.

From these prior events we can determine the significance of Moses' assignment to stand on the top of the hill with the "staff of God" in his hand. Moses' staff had become the symbol of the power of God. Moses' upraised hands were a visual representation of prayer. Together, they signify prayer for the power of God to be displayed—or what we would call intercessory prayer.

As the account unfolds we see the impact of Moses' intercessory prayer. As long as Moses held up his hands—that is, as long as Moses was praying—"Joshua overcame the Amalekite army with the sword." Whenever Moses lowered his hands, the Amalekites prevailed (Ex. 17:11). Moses' prayer was the decisive difference between winning and losing the battle!

With this victory, Moses and the Israelites gained an important new lesson. In the succeeding verses Moses explains "something to be remembered" in the Israelites' expanding understanding of God (Ex. 17:14-16). These insights can be summarized in three points.

First, we must expect conflict. Moses prophesied, "The Lord will be at war against the Amalekites from generation to generation" (Ex. 17:16). The Amalekites represent the enemies of God—the world, the flesh, and the devil. When we are weak, tired, and lagging behind, they will attack fiercely and ruthlessly. We may become overwhelmed by discouragement, depression, fear, anxiety, bitterness, or self-pity. We may be buffeted by hardships, difficulties, and setbacks. We may be distracted, enticed, or ridiculed by friends. We may be diverted by pleasures, enticements, or lesser tasks. When we are actively pursuing the plan and purposes of God, we can expect spiritual challenges of one kind or another.

Second, prayer is an essential weapon in the battle. Moses clearly recognized the crucial importance of intercessory prayer in the victory over the Amalekites, "For hands were lifted up to the throne of the Lord" (Ex. 17:16). As he watched the ebb and flow of the battle from his vantage point on the hill, he could see a direct and immediate relationship between his intercessory prayer and the outcome of the battle. In that battle, as in ours, the difference between victory and defeat depended on intercessory prayer. Without intercessory prayer the tide of battle turns against us. With prayer our fighters press on toward victory.

Third, we learn that when we pray and fight, we overcome. The Lord promised Moses, "I will completely erase the memory of the Amalekites from under heaven." The Amalekites were defeated here for the first time as Moses prayed and Joshua fought. Throughout its history, Israel applied this same pattern in subsequent battles—fervent prayers and hard blows, silent intercession and active exertion. Finally, in the reign of Judah's King

Hezekiah, hundreds of years later, Moses' prophecy was fulfilled (1 Chr. 4:41-43). The Amalekites were exterminated, as God had promised, once and for all.

When we learn to combine intercessory prayer with active exertion, we *will* prevail in spiritual conflict. The unseen forces of Satan will be routed and we will overcome! Nowhere is this more true than in the fierce, intense battle for men and women, boys and girls in evangelism.

Far from taking a lesser assignment, Stu and Catherine have been specially gifted for one of the most demanding. The work of intercessory prayer is absolutely crucial to the success of any evangelistic initiative. Without it, every other human effort to evangelize will fail.

How to pray for evangelism

The Bible assures us that when we pray, God answers. The Apostle John writes, "This is the assurance we have in approaching God: that if we ask anything according to his will, he hears us. And if we know that he hears us—whatever we ask—we know that we have what we asked of him" (1 John 5:14-15).

But God's promise to answer our prayers is given to us on the condition that we pray "according to his will." This means that our prayers are most effective when we pray in agreement with the revealed purposes of God.

At least twelve different evangelistic prayers (or requests for prayer) are recorded in the New Testament. These biblical prayers express the revealed will of God for evangelistic endeavors and become the normative pattern for our prayers.

But it is eye-opening to observe that the overwhelming majority of New Testament prayer related to evangelism is radically different from our own! With the best intentions and with fervor and persistence we pray for evangelism, but with much less effectiveness than we might because we are not praying in the biblical way.

As I see discernible, exciting answers to Stu and Catherine's prayers week after week, I am increasingly convinced that there is far more power in evangelistic prayer than we have realized. But it is crucial that we pattern our prayers after those in the New Testament.

Have you ever examined the biblical prayers for evangelism? Nineteen New Testament prayer requests can be found which pertain specifically to the work of evangelism. From among them we can identify twelve particular requests. Let's look at them, one at a time.

1. Prayer to enlist workers. The prayer that is basic to all the others is the prayer for workers. As we have seen in Chapter 1, it is essential to the evangelistic enterprise that we "Ask the Lord of the harvest . . . to send out workers into his harvest field" (Matt. 9:38).

The urgency to pray comes because of the reluctance of the potential workers. Unlike Jesus, we are often moved by emotions other than compassion when we encounter the traits, attitudes, habits, and associations which so often characterize unchurched persons. We may be repulsed by crude, obscene language. A particular vice, like smoking or taking drugs, may be offensive. We may be inconvenienced or threatened by the sinful traits of unsaved persons and may become angry. In order to protect ourselves—or, more often, our children—we may withdraw to "safer" relationships and associations. As our life revolves around these comfortable associations, we may become indifferent to unsaved and unchurched persons. Or we may simply be too busy raising a family, establishing a career, or building a business to invest ourselves in active evangelism.

But we do not resign ourselves to this unwillingness. We pray to change the minds and melt the hearts of potential workers. We challenge and overcome this reluctance with the prayer: "Lord, send out workers into your harvest field!"

2. Prayer for the Holy Spirit. A second evangelistic prayer commended to us by Jesus is prayer for the Holy Spirit. In his instructions to the apostles just before his ascension, Jesus told his disciples to wait for the gift of the Holy Spirit, who would give them power to witness (Acts 1:4-5,8). In obedience to the Lord's directive, 120 disciples waited in Jerusalem for the next ten days and "they all joined together constantly in prayer" (Acts 1:14).

Ten days later they were filled with the Holy Spirit and from that time on empowered to witness. The Holy Spirit gave them words for their witness (Acts 4:5-13; Matt. 10:19-20). They were embued with boldness by the Holy Spirit (Acts 4:13,31; 2 Tim. 1:6-8). As they witnessed, the Holy Spirit brought conviction on their listeners (Acts 5:32; John 15:26 and 16:7-11). On numerous occasions the Holy Spirit gave direction to the apostles as their witness took them to various places and into a variety of new situations. On one occasion the Holy Spirit provided transportation—lifting Phillip by a swift, direct trip from the road to Gaza to Azotus (Acts 8:39-40). And a number of times the Holy Spirit dramatically heightened the impact of the apostles' witness by enabling them to do signs and wonders (Acts 13:6-12; 19:11-12).

As we will see, the apostles prayed specifically for each of these kinds of assistance in their evangelistic work. But all of these things are encompassed in the great gift of the Holy Spirit. Recognizing that workers in evangelism will need the empowerment of the Holy Spirit, Luke invites us to pray for the Holy Spirit (Luke 11:9-13).

3. Prayer for boldness. A prayer we encounter as we proceed through Acts is the prayer for *boldness.* Immediately after their first experience of harassment and intimidation by the Jewish ruling council, the apostles reported to the gathered believers. Then they prayed, not for protection from persecution as we might have, but for boldness: "Now, Lord, consider their threats and enable your servants to speak your word with great boldness" (Acts 4:29).

It is fascinating that the apostles never outgrew their need for boldness. It would be easy to think that Peter and Paul, with their naturally outgoing temperaments would, with a bit of experience in witnessing, be readily and easily bold. But this is not the case. Even after years of experience in preaching, teaching, and evangelistic work, Paul requests prayer for boldness. "Pray also for me . . . that I will fearlessly make known the mystery of the gospel, for which I am an ambassador in chains. Pray that I may declare it fearlessly, as I should" (Eph. 6:19-20).

If Paul needed to pray for boldness, we can reasonably conclude that *all* evangelistic workers need prayer for boldness. Even for the most experienced and effective workers, our reserves of courage are quickly expended. We need continual doses of fresh courage. Though we may be confident and successful in other areas, we can be frightened to the core in evangelism. The response is not to run away with timidity as our excuse, but to pray for boldness.

4. *Prayer for signs and wonders.* Immediately after their prayer for boldness, Peter and the other believers made an even more startling request. "Stretch out your hand to heal and perform miraculous signs and wonders through the name of your holy servant Jesus" (Acts 4:30).

From their long association with Jesus, Peter and John had seen how healing was fully woven into Jesus' ministry. In their own brief ministry up to this time, they knew the power of a dramatic miracle to attract a crowd of people. On the day of Pentecost thousands of people had rushed to see the supernatural phenomena of wind, fire, and speech in unknown languages. When the lame beggar at the temple gate was healed in the name of Jesus, Peter had the opportunity to preach to the astonished crowd who came running to see the amazing healing (Acts 3:9-12). Knowing the incisive impact of signs and wonders, they asked the Lord to grant comparable signs and wonders as an acompaniment to their witness.

The Holy Spirit does not use signs and wonders with everyone, of course. He persuades persons in a wide variety of ways. But for some, a striking instance of divine intervention will be decisive. For these persons the Holy Spirit desires to accomplish signs and wonders as we become partners with him in prayer.

5. *Prayer for opportunities.* Paul requested prayer that God would provide opportunities to present the gospel. "And pray for us, too, that God may open a door for our message, so that we may proclaim the mystery of Christ, for which I am in chains" (Col. 4:3). He was writing from prison at the time, yet he did not despair of having opportunities to share his faith. He simply prayed and requested supernatural assistance in finding open doors.

In Oklahoma City we can pray this prayer quite literally. As we contact neighbors, telephone newcomers in the area, and find unchurched people in "door to door" surveys, we pray that the Lord will open the doors of their homes to us.

One Wednesday evening, three of us were visiting with Jay and Jessie, a husband and wife we had contacted through a newcomers listing. During our conversation, Jessie commented, "It's amazing that we are visiting like this. We had intended to call and cancel our appointment, but we forgot. And here we are, talking together." For Jessie it was an uncharacteristic response. For us it was just another instance of the Spirit opening doors in response to prayer.

6. Prayer for words. The apostles also prayed for words. This, too, is surprising. The Apostle Paul was thoroughly versed in the Scriptures. He was fully trained as a teacher of the law. His formal training surpassed any of the other apostles. He had years of experience. By the time he wrote the book of Ephesians, he had countless encounters with both Jews and Gentiles and was thoroughly familiar with their objections and arguments. He was ready with numerous scriptural responses, which he could amplify with applications and illustrations of proven effectiveness. Yet he continued to request prayer for words. "Pray also for me, that whenever I open my mouth, words may be given me" (Eph. 6:19).

Our own fears about knowing what to say need not deter us in the work of evangelism. Rather, our fears should motivate us to pray for the right words.

7. Prayer for Clarity. Paul also requests prayer for clarity. "Pray that I may proclaim [the mystery of the gospel] clearly, as I should" (Col. 4:4).

Paul recognized that God's initiative in offering forgiveness and mercy seems like "foolishness" to the unbeliever (1 Cor. 1:18). The way God has accomplished his purpose in the suffering, death, and resurrection of Jesus Christ is totally unexpected. Its availability to us—not by work or merit, but as a gift—is utterly unlike our usual way of thinking (Prov. 16:25). It is a mystery which natural (as opposed to spiritual) persons cannot understand apart from the enlightening of the Holy Spirit.

We pray wisely and well when we, like Paul, pray for divine assistance in communicating concepts and truths which, apart from the Spirit's help, are inconceivable and incomprehensible.

8. Prayer for active witnessing. In his letter to Philemon, Paul praises his friend for his faith and love. Then he tells Philemon how he is praying for him. "I pray that you may be active in sharing your faith" (Philem. 6).

As many of us know so well, the sheer pressure of good, important work often squeezes out the work of evangelism. Our schedules are full. We have plans, goals, and projects that have piled up on us. In our determination to pursue these goals, the work of evangelism takes a back seat. It seems that these pressing tasks must be done and evangelism, sadly, can wait.

But when we pray for one another to be active in witnessing, we help one another to establish evangelism as a priority. Even in a full schedule, we can commit a specific block of time (or blocks of time) to active, intentional initiatives in evangelism. We reverse the trend toward diversion and distraction and restore one another to the primary work of sharing our faith.

9. Prayer for the rapid spread of the gospel. Paul also requests prayer that the gospel will spread rapidly. "Finally, brothers, pray for us that the message of the Lord may spread rapidly and be honored, just as it was with you" (2 Thess. 3:1).

For a time I pestered the Lord with enormous requests for numerical growth. A wise member of our congregation cautioned me against such single-minded focus on results in our evangelistic enterprise. But I persisted until the Holy Spirit communicated with me directly that the answer to this prayer was being delayed until we had laid in place the foundational approaches and attitudes that I am describing in this book. I see now that we must pray this prayer in proper relation to all the others—in sequence with a full mobilization of workers, empowered by the Holy Spirit, working according to biblical principles.

But once we have done this, we can pray this prayer earnestly, appropriately, and expectantly. We can pray and then rejoice in the promise and potential for a rapid spread of the gospel.

10. Prayer for deliverance. One evangelistic prayer is repeated more than any other in the New Testament. As if to underscore the vital necessity for persevering prayer, five different requests relate specifically to deliverance in spiritual conflict. Prayer is the only way to counter a phenomenon that inevitably occurs when we begin to be active in evangelism: we encounter intense opposition. When we are fulfilling God's plan and purposes in evangelism, we can be certain—as Moses and the Israelites learned so early in their journey to the Promised Land—that we will encounter fierce, cruel, relentless opposition.

In Ephesians 6:10-20, Paul says, explicitly, "Our struggle is not against flesh and blood, but against rulers, against the authorities, against the powers of this dark world and against the spiritual forces of evil in the heavenly realms" (Eph. 6:12). When we are not actively engaged in the work of evangelism, these images and comparisons from warfare seem overdrawn—vivid and helpful, to be sure, but not an actual day-to-day experience.

But when we begin to actively work "to seek and to save those who are lost," this passage takes on a reality we have never before dreamed possible. Within weeks and certainly within a few months we discover that we *are* in a war. In our own experience we learn that the opposition is relentless and utterly unprincipled in its aim to disable, incapacitate, and destroy.

In 2 Corinthians 1:8-9, Paul describes the attacks he and his evangelistic team encountered in Ephesus. "We do not want you to be uninformed, brothers, about the hardships we suffered in the province of Asia. We were under great pressure, far beyond our ability to endure, so that we despaired even of life. Indeed, in our hearts we felt the sentence of death."

Their only hope against such overwhelming hardships was the Lord's deliverance. "On him we have set our hope that he will continue to deliver us." This deliverance is possible, he continues, "as you help us by your prayers." He concludes with his assurance of the result. "Then many will give thanks on our behalf for the gracious favor granted us in answer to the prayers of many" (vv. 10-11).

Writing to the Philippians, Paul appeals to his friends and supporters in Philippi for prayer for deliverance. "Yes, and I will continue to rejoice, for I know that through your prayers and the help given by the Spirit of Jesus Christ, this will turn out for my deliverance" (Phil. 1:19).

To the Thessalonians, Paul cites the ever-present obstacles of wicked and evil men. "And pray that we may be delivered from wicked and evil men, for not everyone has faith." Paul recognizes the one who motivates and directs these evil men as Satan, "but the Lord is faithful, and he will strengthen and protect you from the evil one" (2 Thess. 3:2-3).

Though this kind of spiritual warfare is common in evangelism, defeat is not inevitable. When we pray for deliverance, we can move to the front lines of the battle without fear. We can engage the adversary, drive him back, and advance God's kingdom.

11. Prayer of support for workers. Another New Testament prayer requested by apostles and evangelists is a general one. To the Thessalonians, Paul writes simply, "Brothers, pray for us" (1 Thess. 5:25). In Hebrews we also read this direct appeal, "Pray for us" (Heb. 13:18).

This may be the positive side of the prayer for deliverance. It is a request to pray for any and all potential needs that workers may experience in any area of life.

Every area of life affects our capacity as "whole people" to work productively in evangelism. Business and employment concerns can distract. Families' worries can discourage and dissuade. Physical ailments can preclude involvement and active participation. Spiritual immaturity can limit effectiveness. Disharmony and conflict between persons can drain our strength, undermine credibility, and disqualify us for prayer and witnessing.

Prayer for evangelistic workers in all of these areas of need is vital as a sort of preventative measure to maintain spiritual strength and grow in spiritual maturity.

12. Prayer for the salvation of particular persons. Finally we come to the prayer that is often the primary prayer in our repertoire of evangelistic prayers—prayer for the salvation of particular persons. Paul writes, "Brothers, my heart's desire and prayer to God for the Israelites is that they may be saved" (Rom. 10:1).

Out of love for his fellow Jews, Paul prayed earnestly and faithfully for them. He agonized over their stubborn rejection of the gospel message, and pleaded with God for their salvation. His utter sincerity is evident in his readiness to forfeit his own salvation, and to be damned to hell himself, if it would avail for the salvation of the Jewish people he loved.

Like Paul, we agonize over the persons we love who are resisting and rejecting the gospel, even ones in our own homes. We pour out our agony to the Lord in prayer, asking again and again for the salvation of unsaved and unchurched persons in our family, neighborhood, work, and acquaintance. As he does the same here, Paul gives a biblical endorsement to this natural human response of loving and persistent prayers for these loved ones.

To fulfill God's Great Commission to win the world, we must pray with the full breadth and depth and scope of all of these biblical prayers. Our prayers cannot be limited, as mine often were before I did this study of evangelistic prayers in the New Testament, to appeals for the receptivity of unsaved persons, often naming particular individuals. We must expand our prayer to include workers in evangelism. In fact, to maintain the balance we find in the New Testament (where eighteen out of the nineteen prayers are on behalf of workers), we must concentrate primarily on the needs of active workers in evangelism.

As we follow the pattern of evangelistic prayer in the New Testament church, we will have ample workers. Those who are working in evangelism will experience the enabling power of the Holy Spirit. We will find people to whom we can witness. We will proclaim the gospel with clarity and power. The good news will spread rapidly. And the kingdom of God initiated by Jesus will come. May we pray together—in the biblical way—toward that end!

Activities

1. Prayer is indispensible in effective evangelism. There is a direct and immediate relationship between intercessory prayer and the outcome of our evangelistic initiatives. But our tendency, like Moses, is to tire, lower our hands, and cease praying. How can we motivate one another to persist in the crucial work of prayer?

2. Our prayers are most effective when we pray in accord with the revealed purposes of God. These prayers in the New Testament become the normative pattern for our evangelistic prayers. Which of the twelve types of prayer outlined in this chapter have been predominant in your prayer for evangelism? Using Worksheet 2 (p. 202) as a reminder of the twelve prayers, expand the range of your prayer for evangelism. With a prayer partner or in a small group, begin praying all of these evangelistic prayers.

3. Each of these twelve prayers addresses a potential obstacle in the work of evangelism. List the obstacles which these prayers challenge. Identify ones which you anticipate in your own evangelistic initiative. Rather than being intimidated by these obstacles, write out prayer requests which challenge each obstacle head on. With your partner or group pray expectantly for God to overcome each of these potential difficulties.

4. With a copy of your church, class, or group directory in front of you, pray with your partner or group for each person or household. Ask the Lord of the Harvest to send out each person as a worker in his harvest.

3

Sowing in the Dust

I was at my desk with a list of twenty-five names in front of me. As I had done countless times before, I began to telephone newcomers in our community as part of our evangelistic outreach.

The first family I called, the Alvarezes, were already attending a Roman Catholic church. The Barretts were Baptist. There was no answer at the Bean and Brubridge homes. The Carbonell line was busy. The Carters were not interested at this time. . . .

The next family, I noted on my sheet, was from Virginia. The husband worked for the post office. The wife was a homemaker with three children. They had no church affiliation.

I greeted the woman who answered and introduced myself. "My name is Warren Hoffman. I'm with one of the churches in this area, the Brethren in Christ Church. I've just learned that you're new here in town. . . ."

"Yes, we are."

"I'm calling to see if you've found a church yet and, if not, to find out if we can be helpful to you."

"No, we don't have a church."

"Are you looking for one?"

"Well, sort of. We haven't been going to church. But the last several weeks we have been bombarded with material from a number of churches, and we are thinking about it. This is the closest we've come since we've been married."

"What kind of church are you looking for?"

"Well, we don't want one that is evangelistic. Are you an evangelistic church?"

"Uh . . . what do you mean by 'evangelistic'?"

"Well, you know, going door-to-door visiting people. Dan grew up in the Church of the Brethren. And the few times I attended I went to an Episcopalian Church. We could never do that."

"Yes, we are evangelistic. We try to find persons who are not in church and who may be interested. When it is helpful, we visit with them in their homes. Sometimes we go door-to-door. But not everyone in the church participates, just the ones who want to. It's completely voluntary."

"We would want a family church. We have three children, five, ten, and twelve, and we want them to learn about God."

"Our church is primarily young families. As a young church, just getting started, we can't do everything well. So we concentrate on the needs of our group, and one of these is to care well for the children. We have Sunday school classes for them, a youth choir, and special activities at times."

"We've been out of church for so long that we're afraid to go back. We've been married seventeen years and haven't been in church all that time. We don't know what to say, how to act, or what to wear. We don't want to look like fools. We're really cautious."

"If you think it would be helpful, we'd be pleased to come by your home and tell you more about our church. You could tell us your hopes and concerns, and we can talk about them. Would Wednesday evening be a good time?"

"Yes, I think so."

"Fine, we'll talk with you then. Good-bye."

"Good-bye."

In a city of almost a million persons, we found this unchurched family, presented our witness, and invited them to come to our church. They have continued to come ever since. After seventeen years apart from the church, the Corneilles are now among our most faithful attenders.

How did we do it? Was it a happy coincidence? The force of our persuasion? The attractiveness of our program? Clearly, the Holy Spirit was working. But on a human level, it was the result of plain hard work. We spent two hours telephoning to find them. We made another call to confirm the appointment. Three of us gave two hours for a visit in their home. Then we followed that with another telephone call. Our readiness to work hard at praying, calling, and visiting and calling again enabled us to find—and win—the Corneilles.

As you begin to participate, I must forewarn you. Evangelism is hard work. It requires a large investment of time and energy repeated many times over, person after person.

This is not a new discovery. Psalm 126 describes what we can expect in the work of evangelism. In a psalm that clearly applies to sharing our faith, the psalmist tells us, plainly, that evangelism is hard work, accompanied by uncertainty.

When the Lord brought back the captives to Zion,
we were like men who dreamed.
Our mouths were filled with laughter,
our tongues with songs of joy.
Then it was said among the nations,
"The Lord has done great things for them."
The Lord has done great things for us,
and we are filled with joy.
Restore our fortunes, O Lord,
like streams in the Negev.
Those who sow in tears
will reap with songs of joy.
He who goes out weeping,
carrying seed to sow,
will return with songs of joy,
carrying sheaves with him.

In the first three verses the psalmist remembers a time when the Lord intervened in a powerful way to save his people. With this vivid memory of what it is like to be helped by the Lord, the psalmist offers his prayer in verse four, "Restore our fortunes, O Lord."

Then the psalmist adds a phrase that is packed with meaning: "like streams in the Negev." The Negev desert in southern Palestine receives only four to seven inches of rainfall a year. The soil is sandy and the vegetation sparce and scrubby. All year long the riverbeds are bone-dry—until the winter rains come. Then, literally overnight, they are filled to overflowing with rushing muddy water.

With this arresting word picture the psalmist is pleading,

"Remember how dramatically and decisively you helped us before? Do it again, Lord! Restore our fortunes—swiftly, dramatically, decisively, so that we are laughing and singing and pinching ourselves because it seems like we are dreaming. Enable us to say again, 'The Lord has done great things for us and we are filled with joy!' "

Then the Lord responds to the psalmist's prayer with another compelling image. God replies in effect, if you want that to happen, here's how: "Those who sow in tears will reap with songs of joy. He who goes out weeping, carrying seed to sow, will return with songs of joy, carrying sheaves with him."

I can understand joyful singing at harvesttime. I can picture the harvesters swinging their scythes and singing as they work because they have received a bountiful harvest. But as I initially studied this passage, I could not understand weeping at planting time.

I grew up in an agricultural area, working on farms in the summer. Planting, I recall, was hard work. But hard work by itself does not explain the weeping. Farmers are accustomed to hard work. Why would anyone cry when he is planting grain? It seemed like a melodramatic overstatement.

To resolve my question, I consulted my commentaries. But none of them explained why a farmer weeps as he sows. I was stumped, until I thought to talk with persons who ought to know as much about planting grain as anybody—the Oklahoma wheat farmer. I went to four farmer friends, and asked them each the same question: "Why does Psalm 126 say that the farmer weeps as he sows?" Without any hesitation, all four immediately identified the reason for the farmer's tears.

They said, "Because the farmer makes such a huge investment and the result is so uncertain. A farmer weeps because he's taking a chance. It costs so much—and he never knows what might happen."

One farmer described the kind of investment that an Oklahoma wheat farmer makes in his crop. "The cost of land is enormous, just by itself. A tractor costs between $60,000 and $70,000. A plow costs $10,000. A drill now lists at $22,000. When you add all this together, the farmer spends $70 to $80 an acre to get the seed in the ground. If he is planting 1,000 acres, he invests $80,000 just to plant the seed!

"Ideally," he said, "there will be a couple of good rains in the fall to bring up the stray seeds that germinate and sprout. A farmer works the 'cheat' under. Then while the ground still has good moisture from the rain, he plants the seed, confident that it will come up.

"But some years, like this past year," he explained, "there isn't any rain in the fall. The weather is getting colder. The rain still hasn't come. The farmer waits as long as he can and then, finally, he goes ahead and plants in the dust. No rain. No moisture. No assurance that any rain will come. Eighty thousand dollars lying in the dust.

"The rain may not come in time. Bugs and insects may come instead. Hailstorms and tornadoes can ruin the crop. There may be dry, hot winds just as the wheat is filling out, which reduces the yield. There may be too much rain, so that farmers cannot move heavy equipment into the fields. Any number of catastrophes can result in a low yield, say, of ten bushels an acre.

"With prices now running at $3 to $4 a bushel, the farmer with a thousand acres has spent $80,000 to plant it, and another $10,000 to harvest it, for a total investment of $90,000. At current prices, he sells it for $40,000—for a loss of $50,000 in a single year."

He concluded, "That's why the farmer weeps: because of the huge investment and the great uncertainty."

Another farmer made a comparison to help me grasp the enormity of the risk. "For you who live in the city, it's like taking a whole year's salary, getting it changed into nickels, dimes, and quarters, and then spreading them all out in a field. You don't have that money to live on, and you have no assurance that you'll get any return on your money."

From these plainspoken Oklahoma farmers, I learned why a Palestinian farmer, in conditions similar to those in Oklahoma in a dry fall season, weeps as he sows. He invests so much, without knowing whether the seed will produce a harvest. But he takes the risk and makes the investment, even with tears of anxiety, in the hope of a harvest.

So the promise in the psalm is this: if we will take the risk, if we will make a huge investment "up front," if we will work hard in spite of the uncertainty, we *will* reap a bountiful harvest in evangelism.

There are times in evangelism when "rain" is abundant. In a time of renewal or revival the Spirit seems to be poured out on people in a special way. The grace of God is so evident that we can almost see the Holy Spirit working. At times like this, evangelism becomes easy, almost effortless. People respond quickly and wholeheartedly under this special anointing by the Holy Spirit.

But like the Oklahoma wheat farmer, we cannot always wait for the rain. Sometimes—in fact, most times—long before there is any indication of potential receptivity, we must "sow in the dust." We proceed without any indications that the Spirit is moving. We take the risk and make the investment, in spite of the uncertainty, in the hope that, among all the "dusty" people we contact, there will be a harvest.

We can understand how a farmer, whether in ancient Palestine or in present day Oklahoma, plants seeds. But how do we sow in our evangelistic initiatives? What is the investment we make up front in evangelism? What is the hard work we do in the hope of a return?

Finding the unchurched

We must invest ourselves, first of all, in finding the unchurched persons who are receptive to the good news. The difficulty, of course, is that receptive unchurched persons are not bunched in one location. They are scattered all around us, and our job is to locate them among the total population—an endeavor which involves no small amount of hard work, like the weeping farmer.

1. Newcomers. The high mobility in our society, which shows no indication of abating, provides one source of unchurched persons. We may lament the number of persons who move away from our church and community, thinking that the mobility of our population is against us. Yes, mobility does mean loss. But mobility also provides opportunity. People move *from* one place *to* another. Some families will be new in *our* community. While some will have a church background or preference when they arrive, they are at least initially unchurched.

Evangelistic initiatives to newcomers in your community will help active Christians to locate in a new fellowship. More significant for the overall advancement of the kingdom of God, your efforts will uncover unsaved persons who are especially "ripe" for the harvest during the early months in a new home and community. The dislocation and uncertainty of a new home and community often disposes them to be much more receptive to the active witness of a warm, caring church fellowship.

The best way to discover newcomers is word-of-mouth. When people tell you about family, friends and, acquaintances who are moving into an area, you already have a link to the newcomers. You know someone in common—and is much easier to establish rapport.

Next best is often a newcomers greeting service. In Oklahoma City, for $15 a month we receive a list of twenty-five names each week in our target area from the Newcomers Greeting Service, Inc. For an additional $15 we also receive twenty-five names from the area immediately south of ours, but well within the range of our church. With this modest monthly expenditure, we receive a list of two hundred names each month.

In a community that does not have a greeting service, it will be necessary to cultivate basic sources of information. Think through the process of moving into your community. What do people need to do to establish a residence? Typically, newcomers must contact utilities, post office, schools, telephone company, banks, newspaper and medical services. Often they will use moving van companies, make real estate transactions or contact apartment managers. Not all of these will give out lists of new residents, but some will become good sources of information about newcomers in your community.

This may be tedious work. But it will be time well spent. In our mobile society, newcomers are an excellent source of new persons for our churches.

2. Neighborhood survey. Another possible approach is to survey your community with a questionnaire designed to identify unchurched persons. This is a systematic and comprehensive way to assess the number of unchurched persons in a particular neighborhood. It also provides an immediate encounter with the faces, names, and places of unchurched persons.

Unfortunately for many of us, this approach conjures up visions of Mormon missionaries in white shirts and dark trousers moving slowly and deliberately from house to house through a neighborhood. Or we may think of small groups of Jehovah's Witnesses knocking on doors to offer literature and attempt to initiate religious discussion. Some people are overly concerned—to the point of total inaction—about the intrusiveness of this approach. Or they may fear the possibility of a hostile reaction. Beneath it all, there may be an unwillingness to be seen by a friend or acquaintance in what they might critically characterize as "proselytizing."

I can appreciate any reservations you may have, because I had them all! But after two years as a church planter with little apparent progress, I reconsidered my views on door-to-door contacts. Then I fashioned an approach which takes into consideration in an active and responsible way some of the valid concerns.

I learned by trial and error how to talk with people in a non-threatening manner. The concern about intrusiveness is a valid one, but this can be alleviated by sensitivity and respect, both in the timing of our visits and in our speech during our visits. The association with similar methods of cults is also a real one. But we have been able to minimize the damage from this association by dressing differently—neatly and casually, rather than white shirts and ties or suits—and by making an immediate, clear identification of ourselves. With actual experience, the element of pride in my refusal to be seen meeting people at the doors of their homes, while not entirely expunged, has been considerably reduced.

The one obstacle which will always be unavoidable in neighborhood surveys is the sheer amount of work. The process is a slow one, and demands a large investment of time. It is necessary to canvass hundreds of homes to find just a few families. But in our experience these families are often the beginning of a networking process which draws other unchurched families into the church. These in turn bring still others. And the harvest, when it comes, is glorious. In every way it fulfills the description of Psalm 126—first the weeping, then hilarious rejoicing.

3. Family and friends. The best place to find receptive persons is among our family, friends, and neighbors. Studies reveal that for each of us, there is an average of 8.4 unchurched persons among our family, friends, neighbors, and associates at work or school. These existing relationships are natural bridges which persons can cross to come to Christ.

In addition, we can form new friendships among persons with whom we come in contact in our neighborhoods, jobs, and day-to-day activities. As we can establish new acquaintances and then develop the relationships, we build bridges for persons to come to Christ. Anyone who responds to us at an informal social level is a potential candidate for these relational initiatives.

All of these persons, whether in existing relationships or developing ones, are our personal mission field. The key to reaching them is not persuasiveness, but timing. At certain times these persons will be more receptive than at others. Our evangelistic effectiveness among family and friends depends on our ability to watch for circumstances which may stimulate receptivity and to be alert to clues which indicate potential responsiveness.

Often contacts with unchurched family, friends, neighbors, and co-workers are a spontaneous process. It proceeds as church members actively expand their circle of unchurched acquaintances and cultivate these relationships with the intention of winning these persons to Christ and the church. In many cases, this process begins and proceeds at the initiative of the individual believer.

But a church—or evangelistic team within the church—can stimulate and direct this process. Here in Oklahoma City we have noticed that our people bring more guests to our services and activities when we are actively working at newcomer contacts and neighborhood surveys. When we slack off on our intentional evangelism, the number of guests diminishes. So we stay active, if only to stimulate the process of "people telling people."

In addition, a church is wise to plan services, programs and activities with the primary purpose of attracting unchurched persons as guests. This means that the event, whatever it is, will need to be exciting for the people of the church, so they want to invite friends, knowing the church will be presenting itself well. In addition, the event will need to appeal to the interests and needs of the unchurched persons who will be invited to attend. A "major" event of this kind, designed to draw in unchurched guests, every three months (or more, if your church can manage it), will provide a good, expanding list of receptive unchurched persons.

Like master fishermen, we recognize that fish are caught in different ways—with bait, lure, worm, net, etc. When we know a person, we can select the most attractive "lure" for the initial invitation. It may be as simple as the invitation of the disciples when they told friends about Jesus, "Come and see" (John 1:46). It may be a special service or activity of the church which is most appealing—a church dinner or breakfast, a Bible study, a special musical program, a Christian movie, a retreat, a sports event, a family night. The time may be right and the person "ripe" for an immediate presentation of the gospel. Whichever possibilities are available, we decide which one fits the person best, and offer what we have.

Ripe for harvest

Jesus has told us that the fields are white for harvest. And his observation is as true now as it was then. There are many people living close to us who are already prepared by the Holy Spirit. They are interested and seeking, already prepared by God. But we must take the initiative to find them. Before we can go on to anything else, we must find unchurched persons and talk with them in order to identify the receptive persons among them. The more contacts we make, the more receptive persons we will find. The only secret is to persist in the hard, risky, uncertain work of making these initial contacts.

Though this element of risk makes our work hard, I have stumbled on an insight that has immeasurably lightened the emotional drain of these initial contacts. In this initial contact our task is not to persuade; it is to discern receptivity.

Persuasion is definitely part of the evangelistic process. But it does not come at the beginning; it is one of the final stages. Our initial aim is to discern—in an approximate way—where a person is in his or her relationship with Jesus Christ. Among all the persons we talk with, we want to identify the ones who are receptive.

Jesus' comparison with the harvest is a helpful one at this point, because implicit in the idea of harvest is the concept of "ripeness." In Mark 4:26-29, Jesus compares the development of the kingdom of God to grain, growing from planting to harvest. The farmer scatters the seed, Jesus says, and then the soil "produces grain—first the stalk, then the head, then the full kernel in the head. As soon as the grain is ripe, he puts the sickle to it, because the harvest has come."

This certainly has an end-times application. But it applies just as certainly to the development of the kingdom of God in each individual life. Receptivity progresses from one stage to the next until the person is "ripe" for harvest. In an initial contact, our task is not necessarily to "harvest" a person. Interest in Christ may have just sprouted; the person is not ready! Or understanding is still developing; the person is still "green." A particular life crisis may have come to a head, with a full kernel of trouble, but the person is not yet willing to surrender to Christ; he or she is not quite "ripe."

In the same way that a premature attempt to harvest wheat is foolish, our premature attempts to "harvest" potential converts is ill-advised and counterproductive. It may delay the harvest, or ruin the possibility altogether. We must approach new persons with the experienced eye of a grain farmer, looking over his fields to determine their ripeness for harvest.

Persons experiencing change are often receptive. A new home, a new child, a new job, living in a new community, a new school (or having a child in school for the first time)—any of these transitions disrupt established patterns and create new needs. Persons may have left friends and activities and be looking for new friends and opportunities. They may be unsure of themselves in a new area and be looking for helpful counsel and experience. These changes become opportunities to care and serve—and, thereby, to build and deepen a relationship in which we can share our witness to Christ.

Persons with felt needs will be more receptive. Persons are especially responsive to supportive friendship and good news when they are encountering difficulties and pressures from sickness, a serious illness, the death of a loved one, financial reverses, marital problems, child-rearing problems, or substance abuse. Any of these difficulties can be opportunities for caring and serving. As Robert Schuller says, "Find a need and fill it. Find a hurt and heal it."[3]

Friends of converts are often receptive. As persons are influenced by friends and acquaintances who have come to Christ and begun to live and talk differently, their curiosity is aroused and a reflective process begins. When we recognize that this is happening, we can "plug in" to the witness that is impacting their lives—and perhaps bring it to consummation with our own witness.

In John 4:35-38 Jesus asks his disciples "Do you not say, 'Four months more and then the harvest'? I tell you, open your eyes and look at the fields! They are ripe for harvest." Among all the unchurched persons around us, some are receptive and ready. Others have sown, and the hard work of preparation has been done, and these persons, right now, are "ripe" for the harvest.

In some instances, this preparation all has occurred in one place through the instrumentality of persons in a single church. But in our mobile and pluralistic society, this is increasingly rare. Far more often, the Holy Spirit has been working through a variety of people, in a succession of circumstances, often in a number of places, to bring persons to the point of readiness. When we contact them at that moment, we may well be the persons (and church) designated by the Spirit to "harvest" this particular person. At this point these persons have been so well prepared by the Holy Spirit that the "grain" does not even have to be picked. With a minimum of evangelistic skill it drops into our hands.

These periods of receptivity do not last forever. They will pass. A day, a week, or a month may be too long. So we must be alert to the clues which indicate potential responsiveness and act promptly to invest our time on these receptive persons.

In these first contacts, we never know what kind of a response we are going to get. Every time, we take a risk! We make an enormous investment of time and emotional energy, knowing before we ever begin that some, perhaps most, persons will not respond positively, and our work will seem unproductive.

Talking with people in itself is not difficult; we spend hours each day in conversation with people, face-to-face and on the telephone. But when we add the element of risk, the uncertainty of an unknown reaction, and the necessity of encountering these responses time and time again, this work becomes hard. Like the farmer in Psalm 126, we "weep" as we sow.

But only when we keep sowing, in spite of our "tears" of apprehension and uncertainty, are we able to discover the persons in whom the Spirit is moving and working.

Oklahoma farmers have some old sayings with which they encourage one another to risk the huge investment in planting grain in the face of uncertainty. One is, "It won't grow in the bin!" Unless we make this initial contact with unchurched people, how can we ever expect to win anyone to Christ and his church?

Another of their sayings is: "If you sow in the dust, your graneries will bust." That is precisely the Lord's promise. When we sow in the dust, when we sow in tears, we will reap with songs of joy!

Activities

1. In connection with Chapter 1, you have already calculated the number of unchurched persons in your area. Now you are ready to translate impersonal statistical data into real people—with names, addresses, and telephone numbers. Develop a list of unchurched persons who are prospective participants in your church. Begin by listing inactive members. Include occasional participants. As you discover newcomers in your community, add them to your list. Ask persons in your group to submit names of unchurched individuals among their family, friends, and neighbors. As guests come to your services and activities, add their names to the expanding list. (If your congregation has not

already done so, devise a way to register all the guests who come to your services and activities.) Be sure that the names of guests, newcomers, and other unchurched persons are communicated to the person who maintains the cumulative list of prospective participants.

2. Some families are new in your community. Do you know who they are? To find them, you can develop a word-of-mouth reporting system. You may be able to use a newcomers greeting service. Or you can cultivate basic sources of information about newcomers. Use Worksheet 3 (p. 203) to devise a way to identify newcomers in your community.

3. Try your hand at contacting newcomers by telephone. Ask whether the person or family has found a church yet and, if not, whether your church can be helpful. After this introduction, the person will probably respond in one of several typical ways. The telephone guide in Worksheet 4 (p. 204) will direct you in some responses you can make. If you are not comfortable making these calls by yourself, listen on an extension phone as another person calls. Or find a partner and practice simulated calls, using responses based on the ones in the telephone guide.

If the person you contact is open to a visit, schedule an appointment for the following week at the time your congregation or study group has designated for evangelistic contacts. Record pertinent information on the appointment sheet (Worksheet 5, p. 207) and give it to your congregation's visitation committee (if you have one), the pastor, or your study group leader. If your study group will be making the home visits for the first time, Worksheet 12 (p. 231) has some important, helpful tips.

4. As an optional activity, plan a time to survey persons in your community. Select a nearby neighborhood and approach persons door-to-door. Or contact them by telephone, using a city directory (usually available in a public library) or telephone book. Use the opinion poll in Worksheet 6 (pp. 208-210). Unless you need to adapt them because of the sensitivities of your community, follow the surveying suggestions introducing the worksheet.

4

Easiest of All

"When we moved to Oklahoma, we had no reason for coming except a definite sense that God wanted us here. We had no family or friends here. The move was not especially advantageous financially. To make the move, we had to sell our home and then many of our possessions in a garage sale."

Dave smiled and continued. "At the time, I was still trying to stop smoking. I wanted to make a fresh start in Oklahoma without this habit. And one evening on the way to Oklahoma I threw my lighter and all of my cigarettes into the trash basket in my motel room."

A ripple of appreciative smiles spread across the face of Dave's listeners, along with several chuckles of anticipation. His listeners could recall similar moments of resolve and, from personal experience, could anticipate the probable result.

Among this group, one man had not yet made any profession of faith. He and his family had begun attending services, but were still mulling over the claims of Christ—listening, observing, questioning, wondering. Dan was obviously groping toward faith, but was stumbling over reservations that focused on prayer and giving. Yet with the others, he listened, completely at ease, as Dave continued.

"I lay down on the bed, and as I relaxed before going to sleep, I thought of some friends who were also struggling financially. I asked the Lord to provide financial help for them, just as he had for us. As I prayed, the words came to me sharply and clearly, 'You help them. Send $100.'

"I was astonished! Nothing like this had ever happened to me before. I sat straight up in bed, and asked, 'Lord, was that you?!' No voice responded, but the thought remained, 'Send them $100.'

"I argued with the thought. But the impression was clear, and it persisted.

"I was so frustrated that I got up, went to the trash can, retrieved my cigarettes and lighter, then sat in bed, smoking a cigarette, pondering whether this was the Lord speaking to me or not.

"After mulling it over, I sat down, wrote out a check, and sent it.

"Several months later we were settled into our apartment. Our house had sold, but the money for the down payment was delayed in getting to us. At the same time I was astonished to learn that my employer would not be paying me until the end of the second month of service! Although all our bills were paid, we were penniless. We literally didn't have enough money for the next meal.

"So that evening I took a walk to think and pray. I described our circumstances to the Lord—though, of course, he already knew. I reminded him of his promise to provide for our needs. And I asked for help.

"On the way back to our apartment, I stopped at the mail-box to pick up the mail. In the stack was a letter from friends. I tore it open and inside was a check which would more than cover our immediate food needs. The friend wrote, 'The Lord told us to send you this check. We hope it may meet a need.'

"The Lord had answered my prayer immediately! Actually, he had begun to answer it when the letter was mailed."

The conversation continued with others sharing experiences. But Dave's story had been told, and it had made an impact. At a time that was appropriate and natural, Dave purposefully shared a life experience which directly addressed obstacles which were impeding the progress of Dan's faith. He identified with Dan's newness in the faith venture with the account of his relapse to smoking. He spoke simply, in a normal tone and manner. He spoke from his own experience, which no one, not even Dan, could refute. And everyone, particularly Dan, heard this humorous and persuasive evidence of God's power and love, particularly in the areas of praying and giving.

With his simple retelling of a memorable life experience, Dave was contributing to the work of evangelism in a way which is perhaps the easiest and most natural of all. He was sharing a personal witness.

Unfortunately for many of us, the idea of witnessing stirs a lot of fear and apprehension. We imagine scenes of confrontation. In our minds we feel the panic of not knowing what to say. We envision sharp, painful rejection. We shrink back from the accusation of "fanaticism." We cite our timidity or introverted nature, and assure ourselves that, while others may, we could not witness. Many times we retreat from witnessing with the well-worn rationalization, "I witness by my actions."

All of these fears are based on misconceptions of what it means to witness. I am convinced that many times our failure to witness does not come from an unwillingness or inability, but from a sort of spiritual paralysis which traces back to these misconceptions. Freed from them, all of us—certainly most of us—will be able to witness easily and naturally.

One of the clearest and most helpful passages in dispelling the misconceptions surrounding witnessing is Mark 5:1-20, the story of the healing of a demon-possessed man in the region of the Gerasenes.

As Jesus and his disciples neared the western shore of Lake Galilee, a wild, unkempt man came running toward them. Recognizing immediately that the man was tormented by demons, Jesus began saying, "Come out of this man, you evil spirit!"

When Jesus discovered that the man was tormented not just by one, but by thousands of demons, he gave a word of command and all of the demons fled simultaneously. The man—set free—dressed himself and calmly took a place among the other listeners around Jesus.

When the inhabitants of the surrounding area saw the man dressed, sitting calmly and in his right mind, they were afraid and pleaded with Jesus to leave the region. As Jesus and his disciples boarded their boats to comply, the now-restored man begged to be taken along, but Jesus commissioned him for a different task—that of being a witness to his family and friends.

Qualifications

In Jesus' words we see the qualification for being a witness: "Go home to your family and tell them how much the Lord has done for you, and how he has had mercy on you" (Mark 5:19). The man had only met Jesus once. He had heard only a snatch of his teaching. He had no training. His mind and personality had, until a few moments before, been seriously impaired by the demons. His reputation was in a shambles. He had none of the credentials which we normally associate with witnessing. Yet Jesus commissioned him as a witness because he met the one qualification—God had acted in his life.

The biblical definition of giving witness is stated so well by the Apostle John: "That which was from the beginning, which we have heard, which we have seen with our eyes, which we have looked at and our hands have touched—this we proclaim concerning the Word of life" (1 John 1:1).

We often think of witnessing as a slick presentation, memorized verses and, when people counter with questions and objections, an articulate defense.* These may all be necessary for the eventual conversion of a person. But giving a witness is different from all of these. The one qualification for giving a personal witness is to have "seen and heard" the action of God in our lives. As soon as we have personally experienced the power of God at work in our lives, we are qualified to tell about it.

As witnesses we are called to tell what we have seen and know, not what we don't know! The essential ingredients are authenticity and openness, not a doctorate in apologetics.

Essentially, witnessing is just telling a story. It may be about a single incident, in which we describe one experience in which God had a part or did a particular thing. Or it may be a biographical witness, in which we relate the story of our spiritual life, particularly the narrative of how we came to faith in the first place, and how this experience has changed our life.

---

*In its entirety, evangelization involves the presentation of historical fact, along with biblical meaning and the confirming evidence of subjective personal experience. Often it requires a cogent and persuasive defense (or apologetic). But witnessing, as we are describing it here, focuses narrowly on just one aspect of Christian apologetics—the subjective evidence of our experiences resulting from our personal encounter with Jesus Christ.

But whether we tell about a single experience or relate the complete story of God's action in our life, the essential ingredient in giving a witness is to tell what we have seen and heard: to tell the story of God's action in our life. The restored man by the lakeside met this requirement fully. He had only one experience to share. But it had happened to him; he had seen and heard it, and motivated by great gratitude, was eager to tell what he had seen and heard.

Purpose

For many people, much of the tension which pertains to witnessing is associated with the fear that their witness will be ineffective. They are concerned about the results of their witnessing. When they do not perceive any results, they become discouraged. This overconcern about results traces back to another unfortunate misconception about witnessing—that the purpose of our witness is to bring a person to saving faith in Jesus Christ.

Brace yourself. The purpose in witnessing is *not* to win a person to Christ—at least, not directly and immediately. Yes, the ultimate purpose of our witness is to bring persons to saving faith. The Apostle John makes this clear. "We proclaim to you what we have seen and heard, so that you also may have fellowship with us. And our fellowship is with the Father and with his Son, Jesus Christ" (1 John 1:3). But the immediate impact may be less obvious and decisive, as was the case in the story we just looked at about the man tormented by demons.

After healing him, Jesus instructed the man to go to his home and tell his family and friends about what God had done for him. Mark reports his response. "So the man went away and began to tell in the Decapolis how much Jesus had done for him. And all the people were amazed" (Mark 5:20).

The Bible doesn't say that any of this man's listeners were converted. Mark reports only that they were amazed, astonished, filled with wonder. The man's story caught their attention, made them think, and drew them closer to the point of making an informed decision about Jesus Christ. He did not convert them. Yet he fulfilled the purpose of witness completely. With his story he drew persons closer to an informed decision to accept or reject Jesus Christ.

Peter Wagner, along with others, uses a diagram which places everyone somewhere on a continuum in their relationship with Jesus Christ—exposure, attention, comprehension, evaluation, decision, and regeneration. Everyone we contact will be somewhere on this scale of receptivity.[4]

DISCIPLESHIP: THE TOTAL PROCESS

Phase I: Making Disciples

Stage 1   Ignorance of Christianity
            (May be exposed but pays no attention)
Stage 2   Awareness of Christianity
            (Christianity is a religious option)
Stage 3   Understanding
            (What being a Christian implies)
Stage 4   Personal Involvement
            (What Christ could do for me)
Stage 5   Decision (Verdict)
            (I want it or I don't want it)
Stage 6   Regeneration
            (Disciple made—Theologically)
Stage 7   Incorporation
            (Disciple counted—Strategically)

Phase II: Training Disciples

Fruit of Spirit	Fellowship
Service to others	Prayer
Stewardship	Witness/Reproduction
Small groups	Baptism in Spirit
Time in God's Word	Worship
Confession of sin	Church activity
Spiritual gifts	Missionary outreach

Modified Engle Scale, presented by C. Peter Wagner in his course notebook *Church Growth I* (See Note 4).

The purpose of our witness is not necessarily to bring persons to the point of decision; it is to draw persons closer to a decision. Becky Pippert writes, "Not everyone we meet is ready to accept Christ as Savior. But everyone is on a continuum in their relationship with Christ. Our task is to draw them closer to the point where they choose to become his disciples."5

For someone who has never heard about Christ, the witness we give may be a first exposure. For others who have already been exposed to the Christian faith, but for one reason or another have become calloused and jaded, an effective witness may cause them to reconsider the claims of Christ. For persons who have become entangled in various misconceptions of the gospel message, a witness may bring fuller understanding and result in clarification. For the person who has gained sufficient understanding, our witness may prompt an earnest evaluation of his or her relationship with Christ. And for some, the witness we give may be the final word in a long succession of stories and experiences which "tips the scales" toward a decision to follow Christ.

To be sure, we hope that the eventual result of the cumulative witness of God's people will be conversion. But in any particular instance of witnessing a listener's immediate response is largely irrelevant. Our part is only to tell our story, leaving the results to God.

For many of the people in the region of the Gerasenes, perhaps for all of them, the restored man's story was their first exposure to Jesus. Jesus had never been to their region. When he did attempt to come, he was rebuffed at the shore. In these circumstances the man's witness was highly successful. He caught their attention in this first exposure. They were amazed, astonished, filled with wonder. He whetted their appetite to know more. By simply telling what Jesus had done for him, he drew them closer to an eventual decision for or against Jesus Christ.

Verbal communication

It is imperative, too, that our witness be verbal. Jesus told the restored demoniac, "Go home to your family and *tell* them how much the Lord has done for you" (Mark 5:19).

There is a pernicious half-truth current among believers that we witness by our lives. One half of this truth is that words cannot be a substitute for action. The total witness we give is a composite of the way we live and the things we say. Earnest, faithful obedience is a vital backdrop for a verbal witness. The authenticity of our gospel is verified in our relationships and evident in the common experiences and duties of life. When the message we proclaim is stamped on our lives, there will be the note of authenticity that elicits a wholehearted hearing.

But the other half of this truth is that actions cannot be a substitute for words. Unbelievers have an uncanny capacity to see the least little blemish in our character. In any consideration of our goodness—remember, their "foolish minds are darkened"—they will see the blemishes and stains. We can vividly remember the disorder and disarray of our lives before Christ, and are gratefully aware of all the things God has done for us. Defensive unbelievers, however, observing our life, and wanting to justify their own sinful behaviors, will notice all the things God has *not* done. Their thinking will focus on these things, completely controverting the impact we hope to have with the "witness of our actions." While an earnest obedience is often an authenticating factor in our witness, we must recognize that lives will always *appear* flawed to a defensive unbeliever.

Even if an unbeliever does not question our goodness, a witness attempted just in deeds has no value—because it lacks an essential ingredient. There is no attribution. To whom do we attribute our good life? Our good deeds? Our acts of kindness and mercy? Many persons are doing similar things—with lives as good as ours—from purely humanitarian motives. They may be atheists, agnostics, humanists, cultists, or persons from other religions. Their "doing" in itself may be no different from ours. Our social action, political activity, volunteer services, and personal character by themselves communicate nothing about Christ. Unless we identify Christ as our motivator, the only attribution is to ourselves: that we are good, caring, and helpful persons. Persons of various persuasions or no persuasion may appreciate that, but it is not a witness to Jesus Christ. However impressive it may be, our "doing" cannot stand alone as Christian witness. There must be explicit verbal communication. There must be "telling" in a witness.

Sam Shoemaker wrote, "I cannot, by being good, tell of

Jesus' atoning death and resurrection, nor of my faith in his divinity. The emphasis is too much on me and too little on him."[6] Rosalind Rinker writes, "Our testimony must be both in deed and in word. The spoken word is never really effective unless it is backed up by the life. The living deed is ultimately inadequate without the spoken word. The reason for this is obvious. No life is good enough to speak for itself."[7]

Jesus told the restored man to go home and tell his family how much God had done for him. His dramatically changed life provided crucial confirmation of his words. But these changes by themselves, as extraordinary as they were, would not have communicated anything about Jesus Christ.

Witnessing involves telling a story of God's action in our life. It may be told in a few words or in many, but there must be words.

Urgency

Finally, it is urgent that we witness, both for us and our listeners. Though not immediately obvious, this is clearly a factor in Jesus' refusal to take this restored man with him. At first glance, Jesus' response to the restored man is disconcerting. Up until now Jesus has been calling persons to follow him. He called Simon and Andrew, James and John (Mark 1:16-20). He called Levi (Mark 2:14). Among all the ones he called, he appointed twelve to be "apostles" (Mark 3:13-19). So it is jolting to read that Jesus did not allow this man, who was begging to go along, to accompany him and his other disciples.

But as in all that he did, Jesus acted purposefully in the man's best interest. He told him to return to his family and tell them how much the Lord had done for him in order to complete his healing. The man had been restored to health and sanity, but his healing would not be complete until he was restored to society. He was still isolated from daily association with family and friends. To be completely restored, he needed to learn once again to relate and interact in normal human contacts at home. Association with Jesus and his disciples would have been a sort of "halfway house" on the way to recovery. But the man needed, and was ready for, a full reentry into his previous environment. He had come to terms with whatever trauma, whatever circumstances, whatever persons were involved in his deterioration into demonic dementia. So, to effect a full restoration to family and past associations, Jesus directed the restored man to go home to family and friends, to tell the story of what God had done for him, and to pick up the pieces of his past life.

Though the particulars of our own "healing" will be different, telling our story among family and friends is equally crucial to complete our own salvation. Paul articulates this dimension of salvation in Romans 10:9-10: "If you confess with your mouth, 'Jesus is Lord,' and believe in your heart that God raised him from the dead, you will be saved. For it is with your heart that you believe and are justified, and it is with your mouth that you confess and are saved."

The action of both heart and mouth are essential to our salvation. An inward response to God, in which we believe that God raised Jesus from the dead, is incomplete; it must go on to an outward response, in which we verbally declare that Jesus is Lord of our lives. Without an outward verbal witness to faith, our relationship to Jesus Christ is weak and anemic—like an infant born prematurely, which cannot survive without the monitoring, specialized equipment, and constant care of a modern hospital nursery. But when we gather the courage to tell our family and friends what God has done for us, we are strengthened and established in our faith. We are able to face the world of family, friends, and past associations, some of whom may not know Jesus. As we speak, our faith develops strength. It gains resiliency and toughness. With each successive witness, we gain more and more "staying power" in our relationship with Jesus Christ.

At the same time, our witness is urgent for the sake of others. In this account of the restored man, the people in the region of the Gerasenes had no way of learning about Jesus. Jesus had planned to preach and teach and heal among them, as he had done with his disciples in other places. But their superstitious fear kept them from receiving his ministry. True to his character, Jesus did not force himself upon them. He returned to the boats with his disciples and left the region. But neither did he leave himself without a witness. Though the Gerasenes would not receive him, they would receive one of their own—the restored demoniac. The restored man returned to his hometown, and then traveled through all ten towns in the area, telling his story. The access that was denied Jesus was given freely and joyfully to this man, one of their own. And his story penetrated through the whole region.

In the same way, there are persons in our sphere of influence who, for one reason or another, would reject the approach of a pastor, evangelist, or missionary. They may not pick up and read any Christian literature. They may never tune into Christian programs on television or radio. They would never darken the door of a church. They would not respond in a civil way to a team of lay evangelists. But they will talk with us, because we are a normal, everyday part of their lives. Our witness to these persons is crucial. They have no other way of hearing the gospel.

Paul expressed this concern in a definitive way: "How, then, can they call on the one they have not believed in? And how can they believe in the one of whom they have not heard? And how can they hear without someone preaching to them? And how can they preach unless they are sent? As it is written, 'How beautiful are the feet of those who bring good news!' " (Rom. 10:14-15).

All of us are sent to witness for the sake of our own strengthening in the faith and for the sake of those who will never hear apart from us. In the same way that he sent the restored man to family and friends to tell how much God had done for him, Jesus is sending us.

Half the battle in preparing to witness is clearing away the misconceptions which have kept us from sharing personal stories easily and naturally. But even when the element of fear is taken away, we still need to know *how* to witness. What do we say? How can we tell our story most effectively?

In order to develop a personal story (or stories) which you can share with persons when you witness, it is helpful first of all to identify the most satisfying benefits for you in your relationship with Jesus Chris—initially and subsequently. Consider these possibilities, and note the benefits which have been most satisfying for you: assurance of eternal life, peace, purpose, power, fellowship, support in trouble, new perspective, better relationships, contentment, security, self-control, compassion, gentleness and confidence.

Next, draw upon your memory to identify experiences, incidents, events and situations which illustrate your need *before* you experienced these benefits. After you have done this, return to your memory bank to recall experiences, incidents, events, and situations in which you experienced the reality of this benefit *after* you began to experience its reality in your life.

You may want to take time with family or friends for an "I remember when . . ." session to jog your memory. In the mutual recalling and storytelling, you can help one another to remember significant events and milestones in your faith journey.

Once you have identified specific life experiences, you can shape one or two of them into a personal story which highlights the significant difference Christ has made in your life. You may want to write out your story. It is also helpful to share your personal story (or stories) with sympathetic believers who will offer constructive feedback.

Once you have, you will be prepared to share a personal witness—readily and easily. Without any misconceptions about your qualification or purpose, you will be able to act—at a moment's notice—on the Apostle Peter's instruction, "But in your hearts set apart Christ as Lord. Always be prepared to give an answer to everyone who asks you to give the reason for the hope that you have" (1 Pet. 3:15).

Activities

1. In order to begin to develop a personal story (or stories) which you can share as a witness, identify the most satisfying benefits in your relationship with Christ, initially and subsequently. On Worksheet 7 (p. 211), check the three benefits which have been most satisfying to you.

2. Continuing with Worksheet 7, draw upon your memory to identify life experiences which illustrate your need before you experienced these benefits. Then recall incidents and events in which you have experienced the reality of these benefits in your life. If you have trouble recalling particular experiences, you may want to have an "I remember when . . . " session with one or two others. In a relaxed time of mutual storytelling, you can help one another to remember significant events in your faith journey. Your aim in this activity is only to recall stories and incidents from your experience. With brief notes, describe these experiences in the space provided on the bottom of Worksheet 7.

3. Twice in the book of Acts, the Apostle Paul gives his personal testimony. As further preparation for writing your own testimony (after the study of Chapter 5), examine Paul's testimony in Acts 22 and 26. Note the similarity in the before/during/after format. Study his choice of words in light of his statement in 1 Corinthians 2:1-5. Identify the life experiences which Paul shares. Observe the balance between the different parts of his testimony. Note the responses he received.

4. If you have scheduled any appointments with newcomers, visit these persons in a team of two or three persons. Take time to become acquainted. Describe your church briefly. Tell several personal stories as a witness. Invite the household to a worship service or another church activity. After thirty to forty-five minutes of conversation, conclude the visit. In addition, deploy some person to schedule appointments for the following week. From this point on, include appointment calling and visitation as a regular activity in your weekly practice of evangelism.

5

Seeing and Believing

On one of our evangelistic visits we met a young West African woman, Adesua. As we talked, we learned that she and her boyfriend had some church background in Africa. But with the disruption of living in a new country and culture, they had drifted away from active church involvement. Now a staggering number of obstacles and circumstances kept them from attending church.

One was obvious. Adesua was expecting a baby any time. William, her boyfriend, was rarely at home, she said, because he was working two full-time jobs. Adesua had no way to get to the hospital if her labor would begin when he wasn't at home.

Immediately, our ladies went into action. Several provided items for the baby and nursery. One woman drove Adesua to doctor's appointments and to the grocery store. Twice she took Adesua to the hospital because of false labor pains. She also brought her to our informal prayer fellowship on Sunday evenings.

In one of these meetings we asked Adesua if she had any prayer requests, and she replied, "Pray that the baby will come." We gathered around her and prayed. One person prayed that the baby would come soon. Another prayed that the baby would be strong and healthy. As we prayed, several sharply specific prayer concerns came to Wayne, one of the men in our group. He hesitated because they seemed so daring. The likelihood of their being answered under any conceivable combination of normal circumstances seemed remote. But he overruled his cautions and prayed that William would be home when Adesua's labor pains began, that he would be able to take her to the hospital, and that he would be with her during the delivery of their child.

Two days later Adesua's labor pains began—just before William was scheduled to work. He took her to the hospital and went on to work. By the time he finished his eight hour shift, Adesua was in the final stage of labor. He arrived back at the hospital just in time to be with her for the birth of a strong, healthy son.

Up to this point we had not met William. Our only contact had been with Adesua. But these striking answers to prayer caught William's attention. Shortly after the baby's birth, he was available for us to visit for the first time. He noted that the baby had arrived within days of our prayer, and that his son was strong and healthy. He observed that he had been able to take Adesua to the hospital and, incredibly, that he had been present at the delivery. Then he commented, with some awe, "You people sure have power."

By the New Testament standards, this was a modest manifestation of the Holy Spirit's power. But for William, it was an arresting display of the power of God on his behalf. It moved him into relationship with us and, within a few weeks, into participation in the life of our church.

This is one instance in our own experience here in Oklahoma City of a phenomenon that occurs repeatedly throughout the New Testament—the advance of evangelism with the confirming presence of miraculous signs.

Consistently throughout the New Testament, the proclamation of the kingdom of God is combined with its demonstration in casting out of demons, healing the sick, raising the dead, and so on. These miracles demonstrated the authenticity of the gospel, overcame people's resistance, and drew attention to the good news about Jesus Christ. The result was often a dramatic acceleration in the process of evangelism.

This happened so frequently that it became a pattern: proclamation and demonstration. Jesus and the apostles preached the good news of the kingdom of God *and* they cast out demons, healed the sick, and raised the dead. The message was authenticated by the "signs," as the Apostle John calls them; and the signs were explained in the message. The kingdom of God was announced, and its existence visibly demonstrated in this two-fold pattern of evangelism.

In most contemporary approaches to evangelism, there is little concern for this demonstration of the good news. The task of evangelism is viewed primarily as proclamation. With a clear, logical presentation of the significance of Jesus' death, burial, and resurrection, we appeal to the intellect and the will, not to the heart. While we may hope for responses of brokenness—as evidenced by tears, weeping, and followed by a sense of joy and peace—these are optional. The primary aim is for a prayer to occur expressing a decision to believe and act upon a clear presentation of the gospel.

For all practical purposes, we have lost a vital element of New Testament evangelism. We need to be shown that demonstration was normally combined with proclamation as the "prescribed" approach to evangelism in the New Testament. We need to be persuaded that this same pattern of proclamation and demonstration is normative for us, as well as for the New Testament church. And we need some basic instruction about how to proceed in this area which, for most of us, is new and unfamiliar.

Jesus' ministry

Jesus began his ministry with the bold announcement, "The time has come. . . . The kingdom of God is near. Repent and believe the good news!" (Mark 1:15). Then he backed up this announcement with vivid demonstrations that the kingdom of God was, in fact, breaking in upon history. He cast out demons (Mark 1:25-26, 32, 34) and healed the sick (Mark 1:31, 32-34, 40-42). It is a pattern which he continued throughout his ministry: proclamation and demonstration.

This same pattern is evident in Jesus' encounters with individuals. One of the most rapid conversions in the Gospels is that of Nathanael. When Jesus saw Nathanael approaching, Jesus said of him, "Here is a true Israelite, in whom there is nothing false." Without ever having met him, Jesus identified the essence of Nathanael's character. Astounded, Nathanael asked, "How do you know me?" Jesus answered him with an even more startling revelation, "I saw you while you were still under the fig tree before Philip called you." Nathanael was stunned. Jesus knew him! He knew the events and circumstances of his life in minute detail! With two incisive comments, Nathanael is utterly convinced, "Rabbi, you are the Son of God; you are the King of Israel" (John 1:45-51).

In this delightful vignette Jesus never even announced the good news. Nathanael's thoroughgoing commitment came in response to Jesus' demonstration of the kingdom—with two "small" miracles of supernatural knowledge. In this case the demonstration of the good news *was* the proclamation; and Nathanael responded immediately and wholeheartedly.

A similar flash of insight was the "clincher" in Jesus' evangelistic encounter with the woman at the well (John 4). This conversation is often cited as an example of evangelistic conversation. It began with Jesus' unexpected request for water, which caught the woman by surprise. When she voiced her astonishment, Jesus made an intriguing comment about "living water." Perplexed and interested, the woman asked about the "living water." Jesus replied, still obliquely, with an elaboration of its remarkable promise. The woman, curious about his statement, requested living water from Jesus. With the development of this degree of faith, Jesus directed the conversation to the matter of repentance, "Go, call your husband and come back" (4:16). Touched at a sore spot, the woman replied accurately but guardedly, "I have no husband." Then Jesus, with no prior knowledge of this woman, replied, "You are right when you say you have no husband. The fact is, you have had five husbands, and the man you now have is not your husband. What you have just said is quite true."

Thoroughly alarmed, the woman attempted to evade Jesus' penetrating confrontation by digressing into a theological discussion. Jesus cut through her "smokescreen" with the truth and presented himself as the embodiment of God's truth, the Messiah.

Leaving her water jar behind, the woman ran back to the village to shout out the news that impressed her most forcibly, "Come, see a man who told me everything I ever did. Could this be the Christ?" As a result of this encounter, many of the Samaritans from that town believed in Jesus—specifically, John reports, because of the woman's testimony, "He told me everything I ever did."

In this encounter we see the interplay between proclamation

and demonstration. Jesus presented the good news masterfully, in the way we normally conceive of this happening. But at a crucial point in the conversation, he immeasurably deepened the impact of his words with a disclosure of her secret sins—an arresting demonstration of supernatural power. As a result of both proclamation and demonstration of the good news, this woman came to faith, along with many of the people in her village.

Time and time again, Jesus demonstrated the kingdom he announced by challenging and overcoming demons, disease, nature, and even death. These signs confirmed and authenticated his message; in word and deed Jesus inaugurated the rule of God on earth—and invited everyone's participation.

We might dismiss this combination of proclamation and demonstration as the unique prerogative of Jesus, except that we see the same pattern of proclamation and demonstration in the ministry of his disciples. When Jesus commissioned the Twelve for ministry, he sent them out with instructions to do exactly as he had been doing in his two previous mission tours. "As you go, preach this message: 'The kingdom of heaven is near.' Heal the sick, raise the dead, cleanse those who have leprosy, drive out demons" (Matt. 10:7-8).

This authority was not just given to the Twelve. In Luke 10:1-20, Jesus commissioned seventy-two disciples in the same way. Their instructions, too, were to use the two-fold pattern of proclamation and demonstration. "When you enter a town and are welcomed . . . heal the sick who are there and tell them, 'The kingdom of God is near you' " (Luke 10:8-9). Like the Twelve, the seventy-two went out preaching the kingdom of God, complete with miraculous signs. Joyfully, they returned to report, "Lord, even the demons submit to us in your name" (Luke 10:17).

After Jesus' resurrection and ascension, the apostles and believers in the early church continued the approach that Jesus had trained them in during his earthly ministry. The book of Acts is full of supernatural phenomena which produce evangelistic growth in the church.

The first instance on the day of Pentecost was "a sound like the blowing of a violent wind . . . tongues of fire that separated and came to rest on each of them . . . [and speaking] in other tongues as the Spirit enabled them" (Acts 2:2-4). A large crowd was drawn by the sound to hear the disciples speaking in a variety of different languages. They recognized the speakers as Galileans who would not know these dialects. Yet each person heard them declaring the wonders of God in his or her own native language!

Luke reports, "Amazed and perplexed, they asked one another, 'What does this mean?' " Peter stood to explain these miraculous signs in relation to an Old Testament prophecy which anticipated the Christ (Joel 2:28-32). When the crowd heard Peter's bold and incisive preaching, they were "cut to the heart" and responded in repentance and faith. The result, Luke reports, was that "about three thousand were added to their number that day" (Acts 2:41). The supernatural phenomena of sound, fire, and tongues, combined with Peter's proclamation of the good news, resulted in this dramatic growth of the church.

Next, Luke reports the healing of the lame beggar at the temple. As Peter and John approached the temple for prayer, a lame beggar stopped them with a request for alms. Peter responded, "Silver or gold I do not have, but what I have I give you. In the name of Jesus Christ of Nazareth, walk." Then, taking him by the hand, Peter helped the man to his feet. His feet and ankles were immediately strengthened and "he went with them into the temple courts, walking and jumping, and praising God" (Acts 3:8). Onlookers were filled with wonder and amazement, and in astonishment people came running to see this restored man.

It was another perfect opportunity for Peter and again he proclaimed the good news about Jesus. Before he could complete his message, Peter and John were seized by the temple guard and put in jail. But the combined impact of the miracle and the message could not be undone. Luke reports, "But many who heard the message believed, and the number of men grew to about five thousand" (Acts 4:4). Again, this dramatic increase in the number of believers is a direct result of an astonishing miracle and the bold proclamation of the good news of Jesus.

The preaching of the evangelist Philip in Samaria was also accompanied with arresting displays of supernatural power. In Luke's report, "Philip went down to a city in Samaria and proclaimed the Christ there. When the crowds heard Philip and saw the miraculous signs he did, they all paid close attention to what he said"(Acts 8:5-6). The impact of the signs was to compel attention and guarantee a hearing for the gospel. In spite of the interference of Simon the sorcerer, "they believed Philip as he preached the good news of the kingdom of God and the name of Jesus Christ, [and] were baptized, both men and women" (Acts 8:12).

In Ephesus, Paul's preaching and the miracles God did through him ignited a revival (Acts 19:1-20). Luke specifically reports that "God did extraordinary miracles through Paul." He identifies healings and expulsion of evil spirits among them, and then relates an incident in which the seven sons of Sceva attempt to copy Paul's effectiveness in driving out demons. In the resultant debacle the seven impostors were overpowered and beaten up so badly that they ran from the house naked and bleeding. When the news of this encounter spread through Ephesus, people were seized with fear—and moved to public confession and renunciation of sorcery, the almost-fatal mistake of Sceva's sons. The ultimate result of Paul's preaching *and* the dramatic demonstrations of the power of God was a revival which lasted two years and spread through the entire province of Asia. Luke concludes, "In this way the word of the Lord spread widely and grew in power" (Acts 19:20).

It is evident from these repeated instances that Christ's supernatural ministry was continued in the early church, most notably by the apostles. But, it is important to note that the apostles were not the only ones healing the sick, casting out demons and seeing visions. Other believers did, too. Stephen, Ananias, and Paul were not among the original twelve apostles, yet they also practiced miraculous signs (Acts 6:8; 9:17-18; 19:11-12). The church expected signs and wonders. They were part of its daily life.

Like the Twelve, and all of the early disciples, we have been given the commission to make disciples of all the peoples of the earth. We have been given the message: Jesus Christ has suffered and risen from the dead for the forgiveness of sins. We have been given the means: the empowerment of the Holy Spirit. And we have been given the method: proclamation of this good news with accompanying signs. Just as Jesus did, just as the apostles and early disciples did, we are commissioned to announce and demonstrate the good news!

But *how* do we do it? In what measure are these supernatural signs available to us today? How do we begin without presumptuous mistakes and humiliating failure and embarrassment? Without Jesus' physical presence to teach and train us, how do we learn to exercise his power in supernatural signs?[8]

Be filled

The first step is to be filled with the Holy Spirit. Like the first disciples, we cannot effectively evangelize without the gift of the Holy Spirit. Before proceeding any further, we must heed Jesus' words to his first disciples: "wait for the gift my Father promised" (Acts 1:4).

In a precise biblical sense, every believer receives the Holy Spirit at the moment of conversion. The Apostle Paul explains that it is the initial action of the Holy Spirit that incorporates an individual into the body of Christ. "For we were all baptized by one Spirit into one body—whether Jews or Greeks, slave or free—and we were all given the one Spirit to drink" (1 Cor. 12:13). John presents this understanding in Jesus' interchange with Nicodemus (John 3:3-6) and in his discourse in the Upper Room (John 14:16, 26; 16:7, 13-15).

However, while believers receive the Holy Spirit at the time of their conversion, many do not experience the Holy Spirit's presence in an appreciable way—certainly not in any of the vivid, observable ways that we read about in the book of Acts. With the Holy Spirit resident in their lives, they have the potential for experiencing the power of the Holy Spirit, yet they are not. Something is lacking.

It is at this point that the phrase Luke uses to describe the actions of the Holy Spirit is helpful: being baptized in the Holy Spirit. Our English word "baptize" is a transliteration of the Greek word, *baptizo*, which means to dip or immerse. It conveys the sense of being saturated. With an emphasis slightly different from that of Paul and John, Jesus, Peter and Luke all taught that we should seek to be saturated by the Holy Spirit with power to overcome sin and to be effective in witness and service.

To summarize, Paul emphasizes the initial reception of the

Holy Spirit in the born-again experience. Luke describes the ensuing interaction between the individual and the Holy Spirit in which the Spirit's power is evident in his or her life.

For some people, conversion and the initial filling experience of the Holy Spirit happen simultaneously. For others they happen sequentially: first one, then after an interval of time, the other. Still others never experience the power of the Holy Spirit in their lives for cleaning, witness, and service. What accounts for this difference?

At times in the biblical account, this experience happened according to God's sovereign working, without any verbalized request—as with Cornelius and his household. At other times, disciples actively sought this experience in fervent prayer, as the 120 did at Pentecost (Acts 1:12-14; 2:1). In most instances as they are recorded in Acts, the initial filling experience of the Holy Spirit came when someone, usually an apostle, laid hands on persons and prayed (Acts 8:14-17; 9:17; 19:6). Whatever the human instrumentality, the significant point consistently seems to be the readiness or willingness of the believer. This readiness usually is expressed in a verbal request, often with prayer and the laying on of hands.

When believers learn that it is possible for them to experience the power of the Holy Spirit, and request the filling of the Holy Spirit, it happens. They begin, often immediately, to experience the active, manifest presence of the Holy Spirit in any of the ways that are described in the New Testament.

The key is to ask the Holy Spirit to actualize—or release—his power in your life. If you have been born again, you may be filled with the Spirit at any time, even now! All that is required is your cooperation in opening your heart to God, and asking the Spirit to fill you, cleanse you, and take control of your life.

Listen to the Holy Spirit

A second step to confirming signs is listening to the Spirit. God uses persons who will wait for the Spirit's direction, and then act on it.

When we talk about inviting the Holy Spirit to control our lives, that is more than a figure of speech. We are doing just that—yielding control to the Holy Spirit in whatever situation we find ourselves. When the Spirit gives directives, we act on them. If he does not speak, we wait. It is as simple—and for action-oriented persons, as difficult—as that.

We must empty ourselves of the desire to control God, and instead allow God to control us. Our approach is not directive; it is responsive. In a particular situation we may know what we would *like* God to do and, in our weaker moments, think we know what God *should* do. But the key to success in experiencing confirming signs is learning to yield control to the Holy Spirit— and to listen for his instructions and act on them.

The authority we have is not like driving a car with a lot of discretionary choices. It is like that of a train engineer, who operates a powerful locomotive within the limitations of the tracks, at the proper speeds and on specific schedules.[9]

Typically, as we drive to a home for an evangelistic visit, we pray for the Spirit to grant us signs and wonders. Then as we continue in prayer, we quiet our spirits with adoration and praise. Our aim is to break through the jangle and tumult of our own thoughts to a sense of settled peace in which we are quiet before the Lord. When our minds are clear and our spirits calm, we are ready to listen to the Holy Spirit.

Often, the Spirit's directives come as mental impressions, no different from ordinary thoughts. Sometimes the Spirit speaks to us with an inner word that we hear somewhere in our spirits.[10]

Some people experience a mental picture—a sort of seeing in their minds. At times persons feel physical sensations similar to those of the physical ailment they are being directed to pray for. Commonly, we refer to these as "inspirations," "impressions," "promptings," or "leadings" of the Spirit. Whether the Spirit communicates with us emphatically or faintly, our responsibility is to quiet our minds and spirits, and then to listen for the Spirit's directives.

One instance of the Spirit's communication to me was a gentle impression. As I was driving home from a hospital visit one day, on a route different from my usual one because of construction, I thought of a couple who professed faith, but were not attending church. I glanced at my watch, realized that Connie would be expecting me home for the evening meal shortly, and drove on.

A few days later, I was returning from the same hospital along the same route and had the same thought. This time my schedule was not full, and I stopped in to visit.

Our conversation was casual. I don't recall whether I shared any recent experiences as a witness. But I did offer to pray before I left, and asked whether they had any specific needs. They said their daughter and son-in-law were having trouble and, without identifying it, asked me to pray for them. So I prayed for them in general, as thoughts came into my mind. They thanked me, and I went on my way—with no indication that any "sign" was in progress.

When I stopped to visit them the next time, they spilled out their news. Just two hours after I had prayed, their son-in-law had called from California to tell them he had been called back to work. After nine months of unemployment, he was working again. That, they said, was the need they had asked me to pray for, and the Lord had answered immediately! What to me was an ordinary prayer with a timely answer was for them an impressive instance of the power of God.

Afterward, I reflected on the experience. First of all, I had the thought to stop and visit them. Could that ordinary thought have been inserted into the ordinary meanderings of my mind by the Holy Spirit? Because the timing of the prayer's answer was so striking for the couple, I concluded that it had been. The episode was the first small hint of supernatural signs in my life as an evangelistic worker.

Act on the Spirit's directives

The final step is to act on the directives we receive from the Holy Spirit. Often, our obedience in this involves risk!

Until we become familiar with the Spirit's communications, we often anticipate strong and unmistakable directives, accompanied by some physical sensations, in a circumstance where someone is visibly under conviction by the Holy Spirit. We assume that a supernatural occurrence should feel . . . supernatural! When we do not sense anything out of the ordinary, we conclude that the Holy Spirit is not prompting and directing us.

Unfortunately, when we operate by this assumption, we

often miss the gentle interplay between the Holy Spirit and our own natural minds, emotions, wills, and bodies. We want some confirming "razzle dazzle." But as a general rule, the Holy Spirit works quietly, with a minimum—rather than a maximum—of display. Sometimes the Spirit will provide indicators that a supernatural "happening" is in progress. But generally his directives come to us so gently and quietly that we are hesitant to attribute a particular thought or impression to the Holy Spirit.

Our relationship with the Holy Spirit in this respect is no different from a developing relationship with another human being. In the early stages of a relationship we may want to please someone, but do not know how. Yet as we talk and do things together, our understanding grows; we get to know what the other wants. As a result, we can speak and act in ways that will please our friend.

As our knowledge of what the Lord wants grows from the Bible reading we have done, the teaching we have heard, the counsel we have gotten, and our own developing sense of spiritual propriety, we can stay "in the ballpark" in considering whether a particular directive is from the Spirit.

If it is in accord with biblical truth and precedent, then we can "fine tune" our sensitivity to the Holy Spirit by trial and error. We press ahead on the probability that this "leading" is from the Holy Spirit. And we learn as we go.

Remember the story about our praying for Adesua? Her expected baby was already past due, and it was easy to pray for labor to begin and for the baby to come soon. It is common to pray for a strong and healthy child, as we were. But when the thought came to Wayne to pray that William would be able to drive Adesua to the hospital and be present for the delivery, he hesitated. While others prayed, he wrestled inwardly. Knowing of William's sixteen hour workdays, the prayer seemed foolish—and potentially embarrassing. He hesitated to express such unlikely thoughts in a prayer. But mustering courage, he gathered up these "wild" thoughts—and prayed them. And the result, for William and Adesua, was an authentic sign of God's power and love for them.

As we risk in this way, it is wise not to make claims in excess of our own confidence. We seldom need to say, "The Lord told me. . . ." It is much better, and just as effective, to preface our prayer or action with more humility, "I think the Lord may be saying. . . ." Then we may proceed, with others fully aware that we are still learning to listen to the Lord.

When we sense that the Spirit is working, or when the person responds in a way that indicates the Spirit is moving, our initiative is confirmed. We have another instance of the Spirit's leading in our accumulating pool of experience. And we will be better prepared to recognize the Spirit's voice the next time.

For many of us who are practiced in prayer, and anticipate good and often obvious results, the expectation of signs and wonders may only be a difference in words and in degree. Initially, we may only think of ourselves as "offering to pray" in the course of evangelistic contacts, and then discovering later that the answers to these prayers have impressed unsaved persons.

In our evangelistic visits, we usually ask whether we may pray for the person before we leave. In earlier conversation the person may have shared a personal need. Or, as the person talked about his or her life and activities, we may have discerned unspoken needs. Thoughts may come to us while we are praying. When we have been praying for the Spirit to act in power and have taken time to attune ourselves to the Spirit in worshipful prayer, we generally pray "as the Spirit gives us utterance." We trust the Spirit to be working in the midst of the flow of prayer as it comes spontaneously to our minds, and we articulate this in speech.

There may be some immediate indication of the Spirit's activity—perhaps expressed in tears, an especially warm farewell, or even an acknowledgement of particular help received. Or there may be no indication at the time that anything at all has happened.

Either way, we leave the result to the Lord. Supernatural signs are God's prerogative, and occur at his initiative. Our part is simply to be aware of the possibility, and ready to respond to the Spirit's initiatives as they come. We cannot know how the Spirit is dealing with a given person—and ultimately, that is not our concern. Our part is to be ready to cooperate with the Spirit in any way, including signs and wonders, and to leave the result to him.

Activities

1. Throughout the New Testament the proclamation of the kingdom of God is combined with its demonstration. As you reflect on your own developing responsiveness to the gospel, what was the impact of demonstration in your eventual acceptance? What kinds of demonstration were most influential? In the early stages of your Christian life, what experiences provided support and confirmation for your new faith?

2. With another person, take turns sharing your current joys and concerns. Then pray for each other as you would if in a witnessing situation. Apply the insights and suggestions in this chapter.

3. From the stories and experiences you recalled in the previous session, develop a personal testimony. Select as a theme the most meaningful benefit you have experienced as a Christian. Decide which life experiences most vividly describe the difference "before" and "after." Remember, you are looking for specific life experiences, not general statements. Now place them in sequence: before, during, after. If you cannot recall experiences for each of the three parts of a testimony, use an abbreviated sequence, such as during and after. Use Worksheet 8 (p. 213).

4. Develop a "church testimony" in the same way. List the benefits of your church, class, or group which are especially meaningful to you. Recall life experiences which express this benefit. Write out a testimony with two parts: a theme statement and an illustrative personal story.

6

Convicting Power

I was sitting in an ice cream parlor, talking with Brad, and a "war" was raging inside. I knew that Brad was open to hearing about faith in Christ. I suspected—and feared—that this might be a good time to share with him. At the same time I knew that Brad was about fifteen years my senior, on the staff of Oklahoma University, and a Roman Catholic. My message, as I thought about sharing it with Brad, seemed so simple; the infusion of acute spiritual concerns into a conversation so jolting; and the atmosphere in the ice cream parlor so ordinary and secular, that I faltered. While my inner debate continued, I told Brad about a recent evangelistic training experience.

In five days we were taught to share our faith. There were teaching sessions, demonstrations, role playing, and training experiences. Each of us prepared a personal testimony, and learned an outline for a basic presentation of the gospel, along with Scripture passages and illustrations. Since it's hard to introduce the subject of spiritual things, we learned to start by asking a couple of questions.

"Is that what your lapel button signifies?" Brad indicated a pin with two question marks on it that I was wearing that evening.

"Yes, that's what the pin means."

"What are the questions?"

I hesitated. It was decision time—blast off or abort. I swallowed—inconspicuously, I think—and plunged ahead.

"I can tell you the questions, Greg, in an informational way. Or I can ask you the questions personally, and that will be more pointed and direct. May I ask you the questions?"

"Yes."

In the course I had learned to get a person's permission to speak, and now I had crossed that hurdle. I was committed!

"The first is: 'Have you come to the place in your spiritual life where you know for certain that, if you were to die tonight, you would go to heaven?' "[11]

"No, I'm not sure. I don't see how I can be until that time comes."

"Brad, for a long time I felt the same way. Then someone explained to me how I can know I have eternal life. Now I am certain. May I share what I learned this week about how you can *know* you have eternal life?"

"Yes, I want to hear that."

"First, let me ask the second question: 'Suppose you were to die tonight and stand before God and he were to say to you, "Brad, why should I let you into my heaven?" What would you say?' "

"I wouldn't know what to say. If I were a good Catholic, I could say that I've confessed mortal sins, taken the sacraments, and am living a moral life. But I'm not. I wouldn't know what to say."

"Brad, many people, perhaps most people, would be speechless before God, just as you say you would be. But none of us needs to be. God has shown us the way to receive eternal life—and the way to be sure of it, right now. The Bible says. . . ."

Then I began, one point at a time, to present the gospel as I had been taught that past week. Even as I talked, my mind was in rebellion. My words seemed so plain—so stark. They were not flowing under any sense of inspiration. I felt no tingles, no waves of exhilaration. Yet Brad was listening carefully. But how was he reacting inwardly? I summoned my will, and pressed on.

When I finished, I asked: "Does this make sense to you?"

"I have never heard it that way before. But, yes, it does."

Then, having come all this way, I took a deep breath and asked, "Would you like to receive the gift of eternal life?"

And Brad replied, "I'll have to think about it. . . ."

We chatted a bit more and then parted. I was excited that I had overcome my fears and presented the gospel to Brad. But I felt like it had not amounted to much. I had spoken, clearly in response to an opportunity, but as far as I could tell, without any response on Brad's part.

But the next day Brad sat down to type out a letter to me which read: "As I drove home, these questions you asked kept swirling around in my mind. I could not evade them. Halfway home, I surrendered to Christ and received the gift of eternal life.

"Since then I have been so happy, so full of joy, that my children wonder if I have found a new drug. I am on a 'high' with Jesus. I realize that this is a spiritual honeymoon, that I must come down to earth. But for now, I just want to stay here. . . ."

I discovered that night that the gospel *in itself* has power to effect change in human life. Oswald Hoffman has said, "People are persuaded—whether they're university professors or the retarded—by hearing the real story of Jesus. . . . The gospel straightforwardly told and personally believed has its own persuasion."[12]

The apostle Paul gives one of the clearest explanations of the persuasive power of the gospel message in 1 Corinthians 1:18—2:5. Incredibly, Paul cites five attributes which we often consider essential for effective evangelism, then dismisses them as counterproductive distractions to the gospel message!

> *When I came to you, brothers, I did not come with eloquence or superior wisdom as I proclaimed to you the testimony of God. For I resolved to know nothing while I was with you except Jesus Christ and him crucified. I came to you in weakness and fear, and with much trembling. My message and my preaching were not with wise and persuasive words, but with a demonstration of the Spirit's power, so that your faith might not rest on men's wisdom, but on God's power (1 Cor. 2:1-5).*

In our natural perspective it seems obvious that oratorical skill would be helpful. When we think of a good evangelist, we think of someone who has a way with words. One whose speech is halting, stumbling, or just ordinary, we dismiss as an unlikely evangelist. Yet Paul specifically disclaims fancy words and eloquent speech in his presentation of the gospel. He recalls, "When I came to you, brothers, I did not come with eloquence . . ." (2:1).

Similarly, we often cite broad knowledge as a necessary prerequisite to evangelistic debate. In anticipation of philosophical challenges, we want to be fully prepared for a wide range of tough questions. Or we want to impress persons with our logic or cleverness. But Paul dismisses extensive knowledge as unnecessary and even counterproductive in presenting the gospel. "I did not come with . . . superior wisdom as I proclaimed to you the testimony about God." Then he explains the reason: "so that your faith might not rest on men's wisdom, but on God's power" (2:5).

Understandably, we also think that a composed demeanor is an asset in presenting the gospel. A person who is self-assured, we think, should have a definite advantage. A relaxed and winsome manner cannot help but be an asset in a gospel presentation. But in this, too, Paul challenges our easy assumptions. He reminds the Corinthians, "I came to you in weakness and fear, and with much trembling" (2:3). Whatever Paul's secret, it was not in his composure.

We generally think that an outgoing, persuasive personality is more effective in evangelism. We think of an effective salesperson that we know and apply this line of thinking: If Charlie can sell insurance so well, with his ebullient good humor and his ingenuous persuasiveness, he would be a natural as an evangelist. But Paul also dismisses persuasive techniques—salesmanship—as unnecessary and counterproductive in presenting the gospel. "My message and my preaching," he recalls for the Corinthians, "were not with wise and persuasive words" (2:4). Paul was not a "sales" type of person, and did not aspire to be. Persuasive techniques are not necessary for the evangelist.

Finally, we often think that we are more likely to win a hearing when we can compel respect with credentials of one kind or another. Our intelligence, our position, our influence, our achievements, our prestige, or our popularity, to our way of thinking, will be an asset in presenting the gospel most effectively. Not so, explains the Apostle Paul. "Think of what you were when you were called. Not many of you were . . . of noble birth. . . . But God chose . . . the lowly things of this world and the despised things—and the things that are not—to nullify the things that are, so that no one may boast before him" (1 Cor. 1:26-29).

All of these attributes or achievements, Paul insists, are detrimental to a gospel presentation. We have used them in sports, in school, in business, and in ordinary interaction. Unless our thinking is challenged, we apply them naturally and without thinking to presenting the gospel. They are not just ineffectual; they detract from the message. They are not merely unhelpful; they are actually hurtful. In presenting the gospel message, it is counterproductive to rely on persuasive techniques to display our education, to dazzle with our eloquence, or to impress with our credentials.

This does not discount the value of these things at various other points in our evangelistic work. Paul effectively employed his credentials as a Roman citizen several times in his travels (Acts 16:37; 21:39; 22:26-28; 25:11). He drew upon his broad knowledge of contemporary religions to interest the men of Athens in the gospel (Acts 17:22-31). He told the story of his conversion and handled Scripture adroitly as an effective means of persuasion (Acts 18:4; 26:28; 2 Cor. 5:11). And at times Paul alluded to his education, the best available to Jews at the time.

Paul used these aspects of his personal history to establish contact and to win a hearing. But in presenting the gospel, Paul laid all of these aside. He knew that persons are not influenced by these in responding to the message of Christ; they are influenced by the gospel itself.

In each reference to the gospel in 1 Corinthians 1, Paul alludes to the *power* implicit in the basic message about Jesus Christ. In 1:18 he writes, "For the message of the cross is foolishness to those who are perishing, but to us who are being saved it is the power of God." In 23-24: "We preach Christ crucified: a stumbling block to Jews and foolishness to Gentiles, but to those whom God has called, both Jews and Greeks, Christ the power of God and the wisdom of God." And in 2:4-5: "My message and my preaching were not with wise and persuasive words, but with a demonstration of the Spirit's power, so that your faith might not rest on men's wisdom, but on God's power." The point Paul is underscoring, again and again, is that the gospel is a divine revelation, pulsating with the wisdom and power of God.

This means that we must never hesitate to present the gospel because of any perceived lack on our part in persuasion, education, eloquence, credentials, or demeanor. None of these is necessary! When the gospel message is presented—and allowed to speak for itself—lives are changed. People come to Christ. The gospel *in itself* has explosive power to change lives! The heart of evangelism, the motive power at the center of all that we do is the presentation of the gospel. Every other related skill may be refined and honed to perfection, but if we stop short of presenting the gospel, all the rest of our work—no matter how sincere and how well done—will fail. The gospel—the good news about Jesus Christ—is the only effective agent of change in the lives of unbelievers. We must present the gospel!

The prophet Isaiah challenges us not to sidestep opportunities by doing "all but" presenting the gospel. "When a farmer plows for planting, does he plow continually? Does he keep on breaking up and harrowing the soil? When he has leveled the surface, does he not sow caraway and scatter cummin? Does he not plant wheat in its place, barley in its plot, and spelt in its field? His God instructs him and teaches him the right way" (Isa. 28:23-26).

For us who want to be sowers of the Word, the time comes when enough preparation has been done. To keep building rapport with an unsaved person beyond a certain point is superfluous and redundant. The time has come to sow the seed of the gospel message in a person's life. How will we know when we get to this point? What is the seed that we plant? Practically, how do we proceed?

It is helpful to think of a gospel presentation in three steps—transition, presentation, and invitation. In order to present the gospel effectively we must develop skill in each of these three areas. Let's look at them one at a time.

Transition

For many of us, the first challenge in presenting the gospel is the initial step of turning a conversation to consideration of a personal relationship with Jesus Christ. In order to speak, we must pass this hurdle.

Jesus demonstrated a mastery of making this transition. When Nicodemus opened a conversation with complimentary pleasantries, Jesus discerned immediately the intent of his visit, and spoke immediately to the basic question underlying Nicodemus' initiative, "I tell you the truth, unless a man is born again, he cannot see the kingdom of God" (John 3:3). In a different encounter, Jesus surprised a woman at Jacob's well by asking for a drink of water. Then he stirred her curiosity by offering her "living water." He turned the conversation so decisively to the issue of eternal life that he won an audience, not just with the woman, but with her entire village (John 4:7-41). At another point Jesus turned a conversation about bread to consideration of the "bread of life" (John 6:25-40). He bestowed physical sight on a blind man, and then focused his attention on spiritual sight, which the man accepted (John 9:1-41).

As we read these accounts, Jesus' responses seem entirely spontaneous, as though these incisive transitions came to him as unpremeditated insights. While we might aspire to such spontaneous ease, we do well as beginners to consider ways to move a conversation appropriately and sensitively to spiritual concerns.

In James Kennedy's *Evangelism Explosion* training (referred to at the beginning of this chapter), I learned to ask this question: "Have you come to the place in your spiritual life where you know for certain that if you were to die today you would go to heaven?" Then, to probe the reasons behind the answer a person gives, one can ask, "Suppose you were to die today and stand before God and he were to say to you, 'Why should I let you into my heaven?' What would you say?"

When a person is uncertain about going to heaven or expresses confidence based on presumed goodness or religious activities, one can go on to ask, "May I share with you how I came to know I have eternal life and how you can know it too?"

In his training course *Night of Caring*, Paul Cedar suggests a different opening question which is both sensitive and useful. Using the person's name, ask, "_____, do you consider yourself to be a Christian or are you still on the way?" If the person responds, "Yes," one can say, "That's wonderful! How did you become a Christian?" If the answer is "on the way," an appropriate response would be, "I'm delighted to hear that you're on the way. I remember when I was at the same place." At this point the speaker could share a personal testimony and follow with an appropriate presentation of the good news.[13]

The gospel presentation developed by Campus Crusade suggests this transition, "Just as there are physical laws which govern the physical universe, there are spiritual laws which govern our relationship with God. I'd like to share four of these principles with you."[14] Another booklet, developed cooperatively by Youth For Christ and Campus Crusade, introduces the subject of a person's relationship with God with two statements and a question, "You were created with value and worth. God wants your life to count. Did you know God loves you and created you to have a personal relationship with him?"[15]

In his book *Lifestyle Evangelism,* Joseph Aldrich suggests what he calls the Pilgrimage Question: "At what point are you in your own spiritual pilgrimage?"[16] Or the question might be rephrased more directly, "Has your spiritual pilgrimage come to the point of a personal commitment to Jesus Christ, or are you still on the way?" Any one of these questions allows a person to respond in various ways without embarrassment.

As a conversation progresses, the next step would be what Aldrich calls the Opportunity Statement: "Sometime I'd like the opportunity to share four principles which will enable you to understand what it means to establish a personal relationship with Christ." The final step in a transition would be to ask the Interest Question: "Could I share those four principles with you?" When a person responds positively, the next step is to establish a time and place to talk together.

An effective transition is always invitational. We cannot compel a person to listen. We dare not take advantage of someone's politeness or unassertiveness to press a presentation upon them. And we must not manipulate a person into listening by hiding the real subject of our presentation. In one way or another we must request permission to share. Once we have the person's consent, we can proceed with a gospel presentation.

Presentation

Once a person has "tuned in" to the matter of a relationship with Christ, we have the opportunity to share the essential truths of the Christian message. At this point we need to know the gospel message, and be able to present it clearly and effectively. What is the gospel message? A basic presentation of the

Christian message must contain an announcement of good news—at the point of deep, real needs. Leighton Ford, an associate evangelist of Billy Graham, has observed that humankind has three basic anxieties—death, guilt and meaninglessness. He notes that death was the chief anxiety of ancient man; guilt the primary concern of the Middle Ages; and meaninglessness the prevailing fear for modern man.[17]

An effective gospel presentation generally addresses one of these basic, unmet needs. One booklet begins, "God loves you and created you to have a personal relationship with him." Another presentation begins, "Eternal life is a free gift." The outline provided by InterVarsity Christian Fellowship begins with the statement: "God loves you and created us to find our purpose in fellowship with him." Each one tackles a different aspect of human need—a personal relationship in the place of guilty estrangement, eternal life instead of death, purpose in place of meaninglessness.

The announcement of good news may come first or be woven into the presentation. But an explanation of God's purpose for mankind is basic in any effective presentation.

A presentation must also include at least a thumbnail sketch of God. It may present God as the Creator and state that he actively cares for all of his creation. It will stress his love (John 3:16). Equally fundamental, God will be presented as one who is just, who punishes evil (Rom. 1:18-32).

The human predicament will also be explained. Human beings were created to love and obey God in close personal communion with him (Col. 1:16-18). But humankind has rebelled against God. As a race we have rejected his rule and purpose (Gen. 3). As individuals, each of us has turned away from God (Isa.53:6). Our choice of disobedience has separated us from a just God who cannot accept anything evil; of our own volition we have incurred the punishment of eternal death (Rom. 6:23).

But through Jesus Christ, God has provided for a restoration of our relationship (Col. 1:19-20). Jesus came to earth to die—to bear in his body the full brunt of punishment for the accumulated sin of humankind. Then he rose to new life, thus restoring the possibility of eternal fellowship with God (1 Cor.

15:3-4; John 10:10). Now he offers to us the gift of eternal life (Rom. 6:23).

God does not impose himself upon us, however. A restored relationship with him is our choice. To be reconciled with him, we must acknowledge our rebellion; we must recognize our inability to be forgiven and reconciled to God apart from the death and resurrection of Jesus Christ; and we must accept the rule and purpose of Jesus Christ for our lives (Matt. 4:17; John 1:12). In prayer we express these convictions to him and invite him to live in us (Rev. 3:20).[18]

To summarize, an effective presentation of the Christian message must include an announcement of the good news and the essential facts about God, humankind, and Jesus Christ. The presentation should also call for faith and repentance.

With these essential ingredients in mind, select a gospel presentation that fits your "style" and manner. There are a number of booklets available. You may be familiar with *The Four Spiritual Laws*, developed by Campus Crusade for Christ, and *Peace with God*, which is available from the Billy Graham Evangelistic Association. A newer booklet, which is even more appealing, I think, is *Your Most Important Relationship*, produced jointly by Youth for Christ and Campus Crusade. These booklets are presentations of the basic and essential truths of the Christian message.

There are several larger booklets available, which expand on the essential principles with helpful elaborations and illustrations. The booklet *What is Christianity?* by John W. Alexander is a capsule summary of the essence of the Christian faith. In another booklet, *Hope for a Troubled World*, Alexander considers the cause of persistent human problems and then presents the cure: repentance and faith in Jesus Christ. In *Becoming a Christian*, John R. W. Stott has written a brief description of humankind's fundamental problem and the answer of the Christian faith. He also gives specific steps for a person to respond to God's truth.

If you decide to work from an outline, InterVarsity Christian Fellowship has prepared a helpful summation of the basic Christian message.[19] You can work from this with your own explanation and illustrations. The *Evangelism Explosion* presentation, developed by James Kennedy, is built on an expanded outline and provides Scriptures and illustrations for the presenter.[20]

You may want to develop a presentation of your own. You might select one of the biblical encounters in which Jesus presents the gospel—to Nicodemus (John 3:1-21), to the woman at the well (John 4:4-42), or to the man born blind (John 9:1-41)—and tell the story to an unsaved person, highlighting the essential elements of the Christian message as you find them in each account. In the same way that you would prepare to teach a lesson or give a talk, take a week or two to study one of these passages and develop a "talk" which presents the essential Christian message. It's harder to "start from scratch." But it may be worth the effort to have a message that is faithfully biblical and, at the same time, definitely your own.

Whether you select a booklet, expand on an outline, or develop your own presentation, take time now to get ready for a gospel presentation. Before your next evangelizing encounter, examine the possibilities and select a presentation with which you are essentially comfortable. In the same way that a teacher prepares a lesson, or a lawyer prepares for a courtroom defense, or a cook prepares a meal, take time to prepare a clear presentation of the gospel.

Make your choice with care, but do not belabor the question of which is the best presentation. With actual experience in evangelizing, you can refine and shape the presentation to fit your sensitivities. Initially, it is enough to select (or prepare) a presentation that falls within your "comfort zone" as an individual and as a church—and to begin!*

---

*Sooner or later, you will come up against an individual who listens insincerely and deliberately, perhaps even maliciously, baits you with diversionary comments and questions. At this point you may be motivated (perhaps desperate) to learn more about the refinements of evangelizing. For this, I recommend books like John W. R. Stott's *Basic Christianity*; *Mere Christianity* by C. S. Lewis; *Know Why You Believe* by Paul E. Little; *Runaway World* by Michael Green; and *History and Christianity*, by John Warwick Montgomery.

Invitation

Once we have presented the gospel, the final step in the evangelizing encounter is to invite a decision. In the presentation, we have already explained how to respond. Now, as we conclude, we follow this with an opportunity for commitment.

Here, too, we can use questions to raise the issue of commitment. In James Kennedy's approach, the presenter first checks to be sure the presentation is understood by asking, "Does this make sense to you?" If it does not, the presenter elaborates on the original presentation. Once the gospel is clear to the listener, he asks, "Would you like to receive the gift of eternal life?"

A series of questions which Joseph Aldrich suggests is: Does this make sense to you? On the basis of this, have you ever committed your life to Christ? Is there any reason why you would not want to trust Christ right now?

As we give an invitation to respond, we must not hide the cost of following Christ. But no encapsulization of the gospel can contain the "whole counsel of God." In a gospel presentation we are not teaching; we are proclaiming. At the same time, we need to clearly describe a full response of repentance and faith. With persons for whom one aspect is more readily received than the others, the evangelist must be certain that both are understood and considered. In some cultures, faith in Jesus Christ as the one and only way to God must be underscored. More frequently in contemporary North America, the need for repentance must be emphasized. Many "believe," but fewer are ready to obey. In our generation we must clearly and even pointedly insist on the Lordship of Christ.

Jim Wallis has written, "To convert means far more than to experience the psychological, emotional aspects of change through an inner experience. The Bible accent is clearly on a reversal of direction, a transfer of loyalty, a change in commitment leading to the creation of a new community. . . . It is a radical change in the whole of one's life and in all of one's relationships with the world."[21]

When we describe a full response of repentance and faith in our presentation, we will want to lead the person in a prayer that expresses repentance (Acts 17:30), belief (John 3:36), confession

(Rom. 10:9; 1 John 1:9), and reception. John Stott suggests a prayer which includes these elements:

> *Lord Jesus Christ, I acknowledge that I have gone my own way. I have sinned in thought, word and deed. I am sorry for my sins. I turn from them in repentance.*
> *I believe that you died for me, bearing my sins in your own body. I thank you for your great love.*
> *Now I open the door. Come in, Lord Jesus. Come in as my Savior, and cleanse me. Come in as my Lord, and take control of me. And I will serve you as you give me strength, all my life. Amen.*[22]

Persons who pray to receive Christ will need immediate support and continuing nurture. But that is the subject of another chapter. For now, it is enough to learn to present the gospel: to begin with an appropriate transition, to give a clear presentation, and to conclude with an invitation to a full response of repentance and faith. As we do this, persons *will* accept Jesus Christ.

Just a few moments ago, the phone at my desk rang. My wife Connie called to tell me about her lunchtime conversation with Jennifer, a teenager who has begun attending our church.

"Jennifer prayed to receive Christ! I had asked her whether she was sure she was going to heaven and she said, 'Sometimes I think so, but I don't know.' When I asked what she would say if God asked why he should let her into his heaven, she said, 'I don't know.' So I shared the gospel with her. And she prayed to receive Christ! When we finished, Jennifer looked up and said, 'That's beautiful.'"

With that simple reflection, Jennifer summed up the impact of the gospel. It is glorious good news. It can be simply stated and briefly told. When it is, it has the power to convict and convince and, when accepted, to transform. It is a message that changes lives—and makes them beautiful. And all this begins, potentially, each time we tell this good news.

Activities

1. The Apostle Paul insists that we must never hesitate to present the gospel because of any perceived lacks in persuasion, education, eloquence, credentials, or demeanor. None of these is necessary! When the gospel message is presented—and allowed to speak for itself—people come to Christ. Lives are changed. Reflect on the truth of Paul's assertion in your life. From whom did you hear the gospel? How was it presented? Can you identify a "deciding factor" in your decision to accept Christ? What was it?

2. An effective presentation of the Christian message must include an announcement of good news and the essential facts about God, humankind, and Jesus Christ. The presentation should also call for faith and repentance. With these essential ingredients in mind, select a gospel presentation that fits your style and manner. Examine the available booklets, adopt (or expand on) an outline or develop your own presentation. If your group has done this, familiarize yourself with the presentation(s) that is being used.

3. Ask an experienced presenter or a willing first-timer to demonstrate in simulated encounters three different styles of a gospel presentation. Have someone in the group take the role of a receptive inquirer, and start a conversation as though in an evangelistic encounter. Then role play each of the following approaches:

> (a) a "fill-in-the blank" evangelistic Bible study (Worksheet 10 is a possible study guide).
> (b) a prepared evangelistic Bible study. (Worksheet 9 is similar to the fill-in-the-blank study above; Worksheet 11 is a different approach.)
> (c) an oral presentation you have developed yourself (see suggestions on page 96), using your Bible during the presentation. (This, of course, will require preparing the Bible study in advance.)

If you or your congregation have already decided to use one

of these presentations (or another one such as those listed on p. 95), you may decide to role play only that approach.

4. The best introduction to making a gospel presentation is to observe someone else making a gospel presentation to a receptive non-Christian. If you can, arrange to accompany an experienced person in an evangelistic encounter which is likely to include a gospel presentation. As you are able, schedule visits for your evangelistic team in which one or two persons accompany an experienced presenter as observers.

7

Radical Change

When Laura prayed to receive the Holy Spirit, we were elated. But we were not sure that Laura had ever made a commitment to Christ! So two members of our evangelism team were dispatched to visit with Laura. That evening she prayed with them, committing her life to Jesus Christ as Savior and Lord.

"But I'm not sure Laura understands!" Janie observed afterward. "She hasn't had much of a church background. This is all new to her. I'm sure her heart is right, but her grasp of what it's all about is so fragmentary." Janie spoke almost with a sense of resignation, "She needs to learn so much."

As I was parceling out assignments to members of our evangelistic team a few weeks later, I asked Lannie and Janie to meet with Laura for a series of Bible studies written especially for new Christians. The idea was appealing to them. Laura had just completed her college courses for the semester, and it would be easy to find evenings to meet together. With vacations and summer trips, it might not be possible to meet every week. But every week that their schedules allowed, Lannie and Janie would meet with Laura to study the rudiments of Christian living.

Now the summer was over, and I was eager to know how these teachers were getting along. Lannie responded with a burst of enthusiasm, "It's going great! We've had the best time—rich, warm fellowship each week!"

Janie chimed in, "We've had good discussions about the basics and practical interaction about how to apply these truths to life."

"That's been good for us, too," Lannie enthused. "It's

reminded us of great truths of the Christian faith and renewed our desire to practice them fully."

"Laura is growing as a new believer," Janie continued. "She understands more. She has an earnest desire to learn and is eager to apply what she learns. It really seems she's getting her feet on the ground now."

"If there is anyone else who needs this Bible study," Lannie concluded, "we'd be excited to do it again!"

In their Bible studies with Laura, Lannie and Janie had discovered a dimension of the Great Commission which often goes unnoticed in discussions about evangelism. Jesus commands us: "Therefore go and make disciples of all nations, baptizing them in the name of the Father and of the Son and of the Holy Spirit, and teaching them to obey everything I have commanded you" (Matt. 28:19-20).

He commissions us not only to persuade persons to make a public profession of faith. He charges us to "make disciples" who are fully committed to learning and obeying the teachings of Jesus. When we commit ourselves to the full realization of the Great Commission, we press beyond a public profession of faith to guide converts to complete maturity by "teaching them to obey everything" Jesus has commanded.

The basis of Jesus' thoroughgoing approach to evangelism is his concept of the kingdom of God. "The time has come," Jesus came preaching. "The kingdom of God is near. Repent and believe the good news!" (Mark 1:15). When the people of Capernaum, a town in Galilee, begged Jesus to stay with them, he replied, "I must preach the good news of the kingdom of God to the other towns also, because that is why I was sent" (Luke 4:43). Later, Luke reports that "Jesus traveled about from one town and village to another, proclaiming the good news of the kingdom of God" (Luke 8:1). The kingdom of God is a major theme of Jesus' preaching and teaching with scores of references throughout the Gospels.

What did Jesus mean by "the kingdom of God"? It is not immediately obvious. The concept of a kingdom is no longer a familiar one. There may be a few kingdoms scattered here and there around the world; but we think of kingship as an obsolete type of government. As we stir up our memory of history, the primary sense of "kingdom" for us is geographical. We think of a particular land area somewhere in the world, with clearly-defined boundaries.

As the crowds listened to Jesus' preaching, they visualized the same kind of geographical kingdom. With their Jewish homeland under oppressive Roman rule, Jesus' announcement of the imminent establishment of the "kingdom of God" stirred tremendous excitement for the restoration of an independent Jewish nation. Here was a man, they thought, with the power, persuasiveness, and popularity to ignite a revolt against Rome. He could set the country free, once and for all! In an independent nation under his leadership, they could enjoy freedom, relief from this heavy taxation, financial prosperity, health, and happiness! Even the disciples, up to the time of Jesus' ascension, conceived of the kingdom in geographical terms. "Lord," they asked, "are you at this time going to restore the kingdom to Israel?" (Acts 1:6).

But patiently and persistently throughout his earthly ministry, Jesus worked to delineate a new concept of the kingdom of God. "The kingdom of God," he explained, "does not come visibly, nor will people say, 'Here it is,' or 'There it is,' because the kingdom of God is within [or among] you" (Luke 17:20-21).

The central concept in Jesus' understanding of the kingdom of God was not land mass, but "rule." His kingdom would not be established at a particular place, but in a particular people, all those who acknowledge his rule in their lives. Together, these persons would compose a new community distinct from the rest of unredeemed humanity. The distinction would not be in geographical location, but in manner of life. The values, attitudes and actions of persons living under his rule would be radically transformed to reflect the character and purposes of God himself. Beginning in these people, and extending eventually to all who would join this new community, the rule of God would be inaugurated on earth.

For Jesus, the kingdom of God meant the rule of God. It entailed a life radically transformed to new and godly ways of acting, thinking, and relating. The aim of all of his teaching, preaching, and healing was to invite persons to accept his rule in a decisive personal choice, then to allow it to become a functional reality in a continuing commitment to discipleship and obedience.

Sadly, Jesus' full intention in evangelism has been widely controverted by what has been called "the abbreviated gospel." In this approach to evangelism the emphasis is placed, almost solely, on a verbal acceptance of Christ. With minimal concern for an ongoing relationship with other Christians or a significantly altered lifestyle, persons are urged to "commit" themselves to Christ with a prayer of acceptance. When evangelism is so narrowly conceived, the results can be dramatic, even spectacular. But they are often short-lived.[23]

The widespread influence of this notion of evangelism is evident in the results of a recent Gallup poll. In this survey, thirty-three percent of the adults in the United States claimed to be "born again." Another recent poll reports that sixty-eight percent of this country's population are church adherents. But at the same time pollsters report increasing religious interest, they are reporting increases in divorces, sexual promiscuity, and widespread dishonesty in business and industry. If such a large portion of the population is avowedly Christian, where is the impact on society? To all indications, the millions of persons who are professing faith are having little influence on our society—even though, by these reports, they are in the majority! One begins to suspect that an inadequate conception of evangelism lies behind the discrepancy.[24]

Two years ago I led a couple to the Lord. They made a joyous start and initiated early changes in their "partying" lifestyle. But now their relationship with a key discipling couple has become estranged. They have slipped away from church attendance. After some initial changes, there have been no subsequent observable changes. They continue to profess faith in Christ. Yet before long, I'm afraid, they will return to their former blatantly decadent lifestyle—and become another addition to these confounding statistics.

When Jesus commissioned us to "make disciples," he envisioned a process of thoroughgoing evangelism which announces the good news, elicits responses of faith and commitment, and establishes new believers firmly in a godly manner of life. In our evangelistic endeavors, Jesus anticipates "fruit that will last" (John 15:16). The fruit he intends is the transformed life which proves we are his disciples (John 13:35).

"Being a Christian," Chuck Colson insists, "is more than believing in a vague deity. To follow the Christ of the Scriptures inevitably—and radically—alters one's opinions and values on everything from lifestyle, to the dignity of life, to justice, to art, to intellectual perceptions. It involves the totality of our lives."[25]

Our goal in evangelism, therefore, is not simply to invite persons to make the decision to establish or to re-establish a personal relationship with Christ, although this is of absolute importance. Rather, it is to help them to establish basic Christian commitments and lifestyle patterns that will be fruitful for years to come.

Like the great evangelist and apostle Paul, our vision for evangelism should be the full, uncondensed version: "We proclaim him, admonishing and teaching everyone with all wisdom, so that we may present everyone perfect in Christ. To this end I labor, struggling with all his energy, which so powerfully works in me" (Col. 1:28-29).

With this as our goal, we are committed in evangelism to teaching new converts with the aim of full Christian maturity. This will involve initial exposure to the rudiments of the Christian faith and life. It will require spiritual formation in essentials of Christian discipleship. And it will continue with training which culminates in disciples who are eager, skilled, and productive in Christian witness and service.

What can an evangelistic team do to fulfill this aim of solid, productive Christian maturity in each convert?

Elementary teachings

Initially, all believers need to learn the elementary truths of God's Word. In the same way that an infant is nourished on milk, spiritual infants also need "milk." The Apostle Peter writes, "Like newborn babies, crave pure spiritual milk, so that by it you may grow up in your salvation" (1 Pet. 2:2).

This "milk" is described in the book of Hebrews as "the elementary truths of God's Word" and "the elementary teachings about Christ." The normal pattern in the Christian life is for a convert to be nourished by this milk until these basic truths of the Christian faith are learned and put into consistent, daily practice.

Fortunately, these basic teachings are identified for us: "the foundation of repentance from acts that lead to death, and of faith in God, instruction about baptisms, the laying on of hands, the resurrection of the dead, and eternal judgment"(Heb. 6:1-2).

While there may be some variation of opinion about what each of these phrases means, I would suggest that every new convert is to be taught the rudiments of repentance, faith, assurance, baptism, the infilling (or baptism) of the Holy Spirit, eternal life, and judgment.

Unfortunately, many congregations are neglecting this elementary teaching—for an obvious reason. When a church has not been actively evangelizing, most conversions will be the children and youth of the congregation. From "little on up" these young persons have been exposed to the Christian faith in Sunday school classes, worship services, and children's and youth activities. Before they make a personal commitment to Christ— sometimes, long before they make a mature, unequivocal commitment to Christ—they have been thoroughly schooled in the basics of the Christian faith. Once they make a breakthrough to commitment, they quickly leapfrog over the elementary teachings and sink their teeth into the meat of God's Word. Many congregations, accustomed to this pattern of conversion, do not provide elementary teaching for a simple reason: it is not needed.

Neither is elementary teaching needed when congregations receive transfer members into their church membership. Mature believers may be moving into the area or, in an increasingly common practice, changing churches within the same area. These persons have already received their basic training in another context; all that is needed in addition is a basic orientation to the particular emphases of this church or denomination.

But when a congregation begins to actively evangelize unchurched persons and succeeds in winning commitments to Christ, it is essential to nourish new converts on the pure spiritual milk of God's Word. It is unfair to these new converts to wait until they respond to "gear up" to provide for this basic teaching. In anticipation of their response, we must prepare to provide this "milk" right away. Newborn infants are ready for milk immediately.

I personally think that this basic teaching is so important that every church will want to provide teaching shaped out of its own life and vitality. Even the most basic truths of God's Word are shaped by an underlying understanding of the Christian faith and life; and a new believer needs to sense the consistency and compatibility between these initial formative lessons—and the whole of the church's preaching and teaching and living. One such guide is *Life With God: Basics for New Christians,* a seven-session study guide designed for use with a new believer in a one-on-one contact in the home, or in a small group setting. (See Activity 3 on p. 115.)

When a church (or denomination) cannot develop its own materials, a number of good studies are available from para-church organizations. The Navigators have produced *Studies in Christian Living.* Campus Crusade for Christ has published a series titled *Ten Steps to Christian Maturity.* The Billy Graham Evangelistic Association provides a number of helpful materials. All of these resources are informed by an underlying theology, which may or may not "fit" the basic stance of your congregation. But, with this proviso, all are helpful.

In our own congregation we use the seven-session *Life With God* study guide. Normally, we offer a "new Christians" class during our Sunday school and in these classes teach a handful of new believers at a time. The new believer has a week to prepare with personal study. Then with an hour of encouragement, teaching, interaction, application, and prayer, the convert has the best possible opportunity to learn, ask questions, and apply this teaching in the particular circumstances of his or her life.

At times, we offer this teaching in a new convert's home. Each week, for seven weeks, two members of our evangelistic team go to the new convert's home to teach a lesson. In the home environment, a new Christian is free to ask questions, to confide difficulties and to request prayer—in a way that a more structured group setting could not.

In these weekly contacts (and often between them) this teaching is blended with careful and responsive spiritual care. Our teachers listen for questions and difficulties, whether spoken or unspoken. Often they will ask direct, specific questions about the person's progress in basic skills such as prayer, Bible reading, and witnessing. They give encouragement and counsel. They are open and honest about their own struggles. They pray with and for the new converts. All the while, they work assiduously to build relational connections between the new believers and other members of the church. This elementary teaching, offered promptly, and blended with close-range personal spiritual care, establishes a solid foundation on which subsequent teaching can build.

Basic spiritual formation

Second, every church needs to provide spiritual formation for every new convert. "Milk" is an initial and temporary source of spiritual nourishment. The time comes when spiritual children, like natural ones, are weaned to solid food. A church must be as diligent in providing "meat" as it is initially in providing "milk."

It is exactly at this point that the writer to the Hebrews chides the believers who have continued to dawdle with milk: "We have much to say about this, but it is hard to explain because you are slow to learn. In fact, though by this time you ought to be teachers, you need someone to teach you the elementary truths of God's Word all over again. You need milk, not solid food! Anyone who lives on milk, being still an infant, is not acquainted with the teaching about righteousness. But solid food is for the mature, who by constant use have trained themselves to distinguish good from evil." Then the writer concludes, emphatically, "Therefore let us leave the elementary teachings about Christ and go on to maturity" (Heb. 5:11-14; 6:1).

It is expected that new converts, once they thoroughly master the elementary truths of God's Word, will arrive at a point of readiness for the solid food of spiritual wisdom. Having mastered the basics, they will be earnestly practicing the Christian life to the extent of their understanding and eagerly anticipating teaching of greater wisdom and depth.

When believers arrive at this point of readiness, Paul asserts, we "speak a message of. wisdom among the mature, but not the wisdom of this age or of the rulers of this age, who are coming to nothing. No, we speak of God's secret wisdom, a wisdom that has been hidden and that God destined for our glory before time began" (1 Cor. 2:6-7).

Once a new convert is established in a solid, developing relationship with Jesus Christ, that life must be expressed in a sin-blighted world. The societies and cultures in which we live are locked into un-Christian patterns. Anywhere in the world, prevailing relationships, ideas, and values flout prescribed biblical patterns. In our own culture, personal relationships are often vitiated by competition and manipulation. Men and women relate to one another with an undercurrent of suspicion and fear. Within families, relationships are poisoned by resentment and mistrust. Authority relationships are marred by rebellion, exploitation, dishonesty and deceit.

Ideas are also twisted away from biblical truth. Contemporary philosophies such as existentialism and humanism have infused our contemporary thinking with the primacy of "self." In this way of thinking the individual, answerable only to himself or herself, deserves unlimited freedom in the realization of personal aspirations. The popular scientific theory of behaviorism views humankind mechanistically, as an impersonal device to be fine-tuned for the greatest productivity. For many modern thinkers, truth is no longer objective; it is a subjective phenomenon which varies with persons and circumstances.

Values based on these presuppositions are similarly skewed. For many, money and possessions are prized above everything else. Others chase after unlimited pleasure. Some aspire to power with the intent to dominate. For some persons, even acceptable values such as independence and competitiveness degenerate into selfish ambition, jealousy, envy, and vengefulness.[26]

By the time a person accepts Christ and is filled with the Holy Spirit, he or she has picked up many of these values, ideas, and ways of relating from non-Christian sources. These patterns and habits do not change automatically! They have been deeply ingrained through years of living in families, schools, jobs, and other institutions which serve lords other than Jesus Christ. Worldly, un-Christian environments mold people into worldly patterns of thinking and acting.

Only sustained and determined Christian teaching—in the context of a truly Christian environment—can reshape the worldly patterns of relating, thinking, and valuing which still cling to the new Christian. This is why Paul declares so forcibly, "Therefore, I urge you, brothers, in view of God's mercy, to offer your bodies as living sacrifices, holy and pleasing to God—which is your spiritual worship. Do not conform any longer to the pattern of this world, but be transformed by the renewing of your mind. Then you will be able to test and approve what God's will is—his good, pleasing and perfect will" (Rom. 12:1-2).

No new convert should be expected to sort out unassisted the tangle of worldly influences and emerging biblical patterns. Worldly patterns are so deeply ingrained that the new convert is often unaware of their presence and influence. It must be a cooperative effort, in which the most discerning and mature members assist a developing believer to discern appropriate and explicitly Christian patterns of relating, thinking, and valuing. This process will require the best efforts of pastors and teachers to communicate new Christian patterns to recent converts who are ready for the wisdom of the Spirit.

When our goal is full formation in the Christian life, this teaching cannot be haphazard. Spiritual formation cannot be offered "cafeteria style" so that a new believer picks and chooses according to preference. Nor is it enough to provide "healthful snacks" in the form of periodic seminars and conferences. We must provide the nourishing, strengthening "meat" of comprehensive, sustained teaching in truly Christian patterns of thinking and living. This, of course, must be backed by personal, practical counsel in close relationships of personal accountability in which mature believers help newer, less experienced converts to grow out of worldly patterns and into the patterns of the kingdom of God.

To manage this, a church should identify the traits of a mature disciple as perceived by the group. Before a church can guide new converts to full maturity, it must have a clear picture of what it means, practically and experientially, for a person in their midst to be, in Paul's words, "mature, attaining to the whole measure of the fullness of Christ" (Eph. 4:13).

How does a mature disciple among us approach sexuality? handle conflict? repair wrongdoing? live with a clear conscience? overcome fear? How does a maturing convert discover God's will? grow in faith? establish priorities? What are appropriate patterns in courtship and marriage, in child rearing, or in speech? How does a maturing believer witness to unsaved family members? conduct relationships with non-Christians and the state? overcome habits and addictions? grow closer to God?

Once a church is clear on the ultimate aims of its spiritual formation, it can begin to lay in place a progressive series of teaching/learning opportunities which take an earnest convert to solid maturity. Some courses of study will be readily available and easily obtained. At other times, a congregation will need to search for a course of instruction which fills a particular gap in its comprehensive plan. At times, a team of teachers within the congregation will want to develop (or modify) a particular course of instruction to suit the particular needs of the church. In the end, the congregation should have a comprehensive curriculum for basic spiritual formation.

Next, a congregation will need to arrange these in the most helpful progression as a series of courses in basic Christian living. Attention, too, must be given to the format, so that this basic spiritual formation is readily available to every new convert in a weekly class, a series of seminars, a course of individualized instruction, or some other suitable format.

Finally, the church will want to reshape its congregational life so that these courses are central to its teaching ministry—not an afterthought, tacked on to its current educational program, but at the heart and core of its basic teaching initiatives.

As the traits of Christian life and character are built into more and more individual lives, the church community itself will communicate these truths. By their association with the mature members of the church, new converts will learn new patterns of normative Christian thinking and living. Each new convert will grow from both word and example and, taking his or her place among the mature, begin to contribute to the actively Christian environment which shapes every newcomer. As Jesus said, "You are the light of the world. A city on a hill cannot be hidden. Neither do people light a lamp and put it under a bowl. Instead they put it on its stand, and it gives light to everyone in the house. In the same way, let your light shine before men, that they may see your good deeds and praise your Father in heaven" (Matt. 5:14-16). As we devote ourselves to spiritual formation, an expanding community of believers will grow to maturity and bring others to maturity.

Training and mobilization

The final step in the teaching progression of a maturing convert is training for witness and service. Spiritual maturity is not an end in itself. The ultimate aim of our teaching is to produce mature believers who are productive in witness and service. Our ultimate aim is outward—for others.

It is this ultimate outward stance that underlies Paul's directive to his understudy, Timothy: "And the things you have heard me say in the presence of many witnesses entrust to reliable men who will also be qualified to teach others" (2 Tim. 2:2). For the great evangelist and apostle, Paul, it was not enough that converts develop to the point of maturity and reliability. His great passion was to enlist them in the cause of building the Church!

This same concern lies behind the distress (could we say exasperation?) of the writer to the Hebrews. "In fact, though by this time you ought to be teachers, you need someone to teach you the elementary truths of God's word all over again" (Heb. 5:12). The progression of learning in these believers had been thwarted. They should have progressed from elementary teaching to maturity and then to teaching others. Instead, they were stuck at the first level, unwilling to progress. If they cannot manage the second step of maturity, the apostle laments, how can they progress to the final goal of teaching others?

Many churches stop short of this final, ultimate step in teaching. The work of witness and service is relegated to an overworked minister or to a small workforce of harried and exhausted members. These faithful few either wear themselves out trying to do everything, or they default on certain key responsibilties crucial for the healthy growth and development of a church. Either way, they are criticized and maligned.

In the biblical view, church leaders have a responsibility to equip and mobilize the whole church for service. The oft-quoted passage in Ephesians 4, punctuated more accurately in recent versions of the Bible, reads, "It was he who gave some to be apostles, some to be prophets, some to be evangelists, and some to be pastors and teachers, to prepare God's people for works of service, so that the body of Christ may be built up" (Eph. 4:11-12). The primary work of church leaders is one of preparation—to train and equip *all* of God's people for works of service. Then, with the church's workforce fully deployed, the body of Christ can be built up, as it should be, to full unity and to the full maturity of Christ.

Courses of instruction are helpful for training workers to pray, encourage, evangelize, or teach. When this instruction is clear, biblical, practical, relevant, and manageable, it allays fears, gives guidance, prepares for unexpected contingencies, develops commonality, and creates *esprit de corps*.

In evangelism, a number of courses are getting widespread usage. James Kennedy's *Evangelism Explosion* is helpful in equipping persons to give a gospel presentation. The GRADE (Growth Resulting After Discipleship Evangelism) program, developed by the Wesleyan Church, does an excellent job of integrating the components of evangelism into a team effort for prayer, encouragement, evangelizing, and teaching. *Night of Caring*, a training program developed by Dr. Paul Cedar and distributed by Dynacom Communications, does an excellent job of preparing persons in a sensitive, relational approach to weekly evangelistic visitation. One of these, or another with which you are familiar will be a helpful "centerpiece" for leaders who desire to equip persons for witness and service.[27]

The best use of any of these approaches is in close formation relationships. In his classic on evangelism, *The Master Plan of Evangelism*, Robert Coleman describes Jesus' use of this most-effective-of-all means of evangelistic preparation. Without neglecting the masses, Jesus selected a few who were willing to learn, and concentrated his efforts on them. He trained these men. Though he used times of formal instruction, he taught these men primarily through his constant association with them. In his words and work, he demonstrated the Father's will. He taught constantly in the course of their daily activities. He assigned responsibilities to the disciples so that they could learn from their experience. He reviewed their work and analyzed their successes and failures with them, and after three full years of this intensive, close-range training, these men were ready for their apostolic task.[28]

In doing this, Jesus established a pattern for the early church. In the same way that Jesus trained his disciples, Barnabas trained Paul and Paul trained Timothy. Apparently, there was a similar formation relationship between Peter and Mark. According to church tradition, John taught Polycarp and Polycarp, before his life ended in martyrdom, Irenaeus and Papias in the same close-range manner.[29]

These formation relationships entailed a degree of personal direction beyond normal pastoring. Much of the training occurred in time spent together, with the person giving formation seeking to teach by example. The relationship between the two was deep, close, and personal—paralleling the relationship between a father and a son.

While some churches may profitably apply this approach throughout the discipling process, this intensive approach has the greatest potential in training workers and leaders. When a good training course is blended with close formation relationships, the results can be a dramatic duplication (and thus an expansion) of one's own character and work. Results are not necessarily fast, but they are sure and solid. As Jesus said, "A student is not above his teacher, but everyone who is fully trained will be like his teacher" (Luke 6:40).

Without question, Jesus' message is a radical one. The good news he announced (and the response he invited) was not a modest mental, mystical, spiritual, or attitudinal adjustment. He asserted radical, even disruptive, change in every conceivable human circumstance as the inevitable culmination of entrance into his kingdom and submission to his rule. A commitment to him was the beginning—and just the beginning—of a dynamic of lifelong change as a disciple was conformed, more and more fully, into Jesus' own character and work. Jesus invited persons to enter into the kingdom of God—to submit to his rule in every area of his living. And when he transferred the continuation of his work to his apostles, Jesus commanded that they continue the full extent of his work, teaching successive generations of disciples to obey everything he had commanded. This, he declared, was part and parcel of the work of making disciples.

As we emulate Jesus in obedience to his command, we must press beyond an initial commitment, however sincere, to the full realization of the rule of Christ in a radically changed life. For this we must give ourselves to the task of teaching as part of the full work of evangelization. We begin with the basics, continue with the radical wisdom of maturity, and advance to disciples fully trained in witness and service. Then, and only then, is the work of authentic evangelism complete!

Activities _____

1. In order to teach new converts with the aim of full Christian maturity, a church must identify the traits of a mature disciple. In your estimation, what traits, skills, convictions and practices are characteristic of a mature disciple? (Be specific.)

2. Once a church is clear on the ultimate aims of its spiritual formation, it can plan teaching/learning opportunities which guide converts to full maturity. In what setting do converts in your group learn to put the basics of Christian living into consistent, daily practice? How does your church provide comprehensive teaching in Christian patterns of thinking and living? In what ways are persons being trained for witness and service?

3. With a partner, practice teaching a session of "new Christians" classes with one taking the role of teacher and the other of learner. Midway through the session, exchange roles and continue. If your church does not suggest materials, I recommend contacting the publisher of this book for a sample copy of *Life With God: Basics for New Christians*. (Write to Evangel Publishing, P. O. Box 189, Nappanee, IN 46550; telephone 1-800-822-5919.)

4. As persons in your evangelistic contacts respond to gospel presentations with professions of faith, arrange for two persons to meet with them regularly at the time of your normal evangelistic work for your "new Christians" Bible study. Continue through the required number of weeks until a study is complete.

8

Going the Distance

Slumped into our easy chair was a beaten man. His shoulders sagged. His face was drawn. His new faith had burst and his hopes had fallen with a sickening thud.

We had met Carl over a year before through a door-to-door survey. He greeted us effusively that day, "It's funny you should come by today, because just last night I decided I'm not going to drink any more. Of course, I won't drink any less!"

Carl was brash and personable. In the Bible study that developed from this initial conversation, he entertained us with his "off the wall" humor. Yet sometimes it seemed that the real Carl was hiding behind the jokes.

Then one night his joking stopped abruptly. Carl slammed his Bible shut and announced, "We can't study this! Our home is in a shambles. Our lives are a mess. And it's getting worse all the time. I can't pretend to study this Bible when everything in my life contradicts it."

The conflict and mistrust hidden behind the humor spilled out in a bitter exchange of accusations. As Carl and his wife stormed at one another, I wondered, "Is there hope?"

The following week the conflict broke out, only this time (I couldn't have imagined this the week before) it was worse! I listened, almost overwhelmed by the complexity and depth of mutual hurt.

The next week was the same—and the next and the next. Finally, at the end of another turbulent interchange, Carl said, "I can't handle this on my own. I need to be in church. Will you pray that I will be there on Sunday?" I assured Carl I would pray and asked Charlene how I could pray for her. "I have a sharp pain in my stomach," she said. "I think it's cancer."

We drew together and held hands. I prayed that Carl would come to church and asked the Lord to release Charlene from whatever was causing the pain in her stomach. Then I went home.

The next morning I got a phone call from Carl. "Warren, after you left last night, Charlene started to drink again. She drank all through the night. When I got up at five in the morning, she was sitting at the kitchen table crying, 'Carl, I need help. Get me help.' I called Alcoholics Anonymous and they recommended a rehabilitation center. I just got back from taking her there. We've both been drinking far too much. I've been able to keep functioning, but Charlene hasn't. She would never admit the problem was booze. But now she has, and she's getting help. I've just flushed all of my liquor down the toilet. We're headed in the right direction now. I'll see you in church Sunday. Bye."

On Sunday Carl was at church. He described the turmoil in their home, identified the culprit as alcohol, told of the events of the past few days, and requested prayer. We gathered around Carl and prayed. In the weeks that followed we continued to pray, to care, to visit and to love in all the ways we knew.

In time it became clear that Carl and Charlene's commitment to change was also a commitment to Christ and his Church. When Charlene completed the six weeks at the rehabilitation center, she returned home. Daring to face a new group of people all aware of her struggle, she also came to church.

The turnabout was determined and complete. Both stopped drinking. Carl quit smoking. Not long afterward, he began to tithe. At every opportunity Carl would describe the impact of having "God in his life"—with his usual gusto and humor. It was evident to everyone that their lives were marvelously and dramatically changing.

Now, eight months later, Carl sat slumped in the chair across from me. Under pressure from continuing family conflict, Charlene had taken a drink. Once started, she slid quickly into hopelessness and despair. She would not, and could not, stop drinking. Now she was gone, in a powerful sports car with credit cards—drinking and driving.

The new life Carl and Charlene had begun with such high

hopes eight months before was in a shambles. This time catastrophe was even worse because now they had tried everything, even Christ. Nothing had worked. Their hopes were dashed, smashed, gone.

Yet even in his despair, Carl had come to us. However tenuously, he was hanging on to a thread of faith. We listened, comforted, and counseled. We countered his despair with our hope, his readiness to give up with our perseverance, his "mountain" with our "mustard seed" of faith. And we prayed together.

By the time we finished, the shadow on his face had disappeared. He breathed deeply, squared his shoulders, and stood. He was subdued (a rare demeanor for Carl), but at peace. He thanked us and left with a sufficient measure of hope, faith, and determination to "hang on."

When the congregation learned of Charlene's setback, they rallied to help. One of the ladies baked lasagna for Carl and the children. One man fasted and prayed for seven days. Everyone supported and encouraged Carl as he continued to worship with us. Once she returned home, persons continued to reach out to Charlene with a gentle, unintrusive persistence.

In the months that followed, Charlene renewed her fight against alcoholism. Her recovery was painfully slow. But this time, as she drew upon the power and presence of God, she overcame her addiction. Her victory was decisive and complete.

Now Carl and Charlene are actively working in the congregation. Carl has taught our teens and served on the building committee. Charlene teaches a class and directs our Sunday school. Both share their testimony with joy. They are bringing persons to Christ and the church. Like all of us, Carl and Charlene continue to encounter problems. At times their faith and zeal sag. But now there is a new resiliency, born of experience, that buoys them up and renews their perspective.

As I reflect upon their journey these past years, I marvel at their initial recommitment to Christ. Even more, I savor their recovery from alcoholism and their development toward a sturdy, resilient faith.

We did not do much to bring them to their initial decision. The sheer agony in their lives was sufficient for that. But we did provide the comfort, support, guidance, assistance, counsel, and caring helpfulness which sustained that decision and nurtured it to a living reality.

One of the crucial ingredients in the work of evangelism is encouragement. Many people "make a start," but fewer "go the distance." The ones who do often endure because of encouragement.

Proclamation and encouragement

When the Holy Spirit appointed the first missionary team, he brought together two singularly gifted men. Among the prophets and teachers of the newly established church at Antioch, the Holy Spirit singled out Paul and Barnabas to blend their gifts in missionary evangelism (Acts 13:1-3).

Though many gifts are evident in Paul's subsequent ministry, one was already evident. He preached, powerfully and persuasively, that Jesus is the Christ (Acts 9:22). In Paul's own later reflection, this aspect of his giftedness was dominant in his ministry. He writes to the Ephesians, "Although I am less than the least of all God's people, this grace was given me: to preach to the Gentiles the unsearchable riches of Christ, and to make plain to everyone the administration of this mystery" (Eph. 3:8-9; also see verses 6-7). At times Paul healed, drove out demons, prophesied, taught, and administered churches. But, above all, Paul was gifted by the Holy Spirit to proclaim the gospel with convincing proofs and compelling clarity.

Barnabas was suited for missionary service by giftedness of a different kind. His life and ministry were characterized by generosity (Acts 4:36-37) and an aptness to teach (Acts 11:26). He was respected by the apostles and other church leaders as a "good man, full of the Holy Spirit and faith" (Acts 11:24). Yet his primary gift was the gift of encouragement. This gift was so deeply imprinted on his life that, though his given name was Joseph, the apostles called him "Barnabas (which means Son of Encouragement)" (Acts 4:36).

The first missionary team, assigned by none other than the Holy Spirit, brought together a proclaimer and an encourager (Acts 13:2). These two gifts, it would seem, are essential in evangelism.

As the story of this first missionary journey unfolds, we see the interplay of these two gifts in the work of evangelism. At Salamis, their first stop, Paul and Barnabas "proclaimed the word of God in the Jewish synagogues" (Acts 13:5). Next, they traveled to Pisidian Antioch where the elders of the synagogue said, "Brothers, if you have a message of encouragement for the people, please speak" (Acts 13:15). In response, Paul proclaimed the message about Jesus as the Christ (Acts 13:16-41). As the congregation was dismissed, many of the Jews and devout converts to Judaism followed Paul and Barnabas, who talked with them and urged them to continue in the grace of God—an endeavor of encouragement! (Acts 13:43). After the word of God had spread throughout the surrounding region, hostile Jews stirred up persecution against Paul and Barnabas, and the two apostles traveled on to Iconium, Lystra, and Derbe preaching the good news and winning a large number of disciples. Dogged by persecution, Barnabas and Saul left Derbe and returned to the cities where they had preached earlier, "strengthening the disciples and encouraging them to remain true to the faith" (Acts 14:21).

When the aim of evangelism is to make disciples who live in faith and obedience, encouragement is an indispensable aspect of evangelism. Ongoing encouragement establishes new believers in a pattern of active discipleship. It steadies them when they are buffeted by opposition and difficulties. It is the impetus for continuing growth and development in the Christian life and walk.

Barnabas, the encourager

One way to understand the work of encouragement is to look closely at Barnabas as an encourager. It is a fascinating and enlightening study to trace the activities of Barnabas through the New Testament and to observe the ways he expresses his gift of encouragement in the work of evangelism.

1. Comforting and challenging. The first trait of an encourager is evident in Barnabas' nickname, "Son of Encouragement" (Acts 4:36). The root word for "encouragement" in the Greek language is *parakaleo,* a compound of the words "beside" and "to call." An encourager is one who is called to the side of another, one who gives comfort.

But there is another dimension of meaning in the word *parakaleo*. One can also be called to the side of another to urge or exhort. In this aspect of its meaning, the encourager is one who challenges, one who rouses to action.

Encouragement therefore is expressed in both comfort and challenge. As the need requires, an encourager is tender or tough. At one time an encourager may give a pat on the back. At another, a kick in the pants![30]

In whatever way will be most helpful, the encourager motivates another disciple. The aim in all that is done is to provide whatever is needed for the growth and development of another disciple.

2. Good listening. The next time we encounter Barnabas, he is interceding with the apostles for Saul (Acts 9:26-27). Though this young firebrand had reportedly renounced his raging persecution of the church, all the other believers were afraid of him. But Barnabas went to Saul, listened to his story and discerned its authenticity. Then he retold the story accurately and sympathetically to the apostles. He was able to do this because of another trait of an encourager: he was a good listener.

Whether by nature or by practice, Barnabas had learned the art of listening. He knew that "the heart of the discerning acquires knowledge; the ears of the wise seek it out" (Prov. 18:15). Laying aside whatever preconceptions he may have had, Barnabas listened attentively, actively seeking to understand what young Saul was saying.

To listen well, like Barnabas, we concentrate our full attention on the speaker. We listen for main ideas. We pay attention to facts supporting the main ideas. Sometimes we ask for clarification. At other times we repeat the speaker's idea in our own words—to check whether we understand correctly. All the while, we resist the temptation to draw premature conclusions. As good listeners we will hold whatever conclusions we may have as tentative ones until we have all the facts. Only then will we be able to clearly discern the particular needs of the person and make an accurate diagnosis.

As we develop skill in listening, we will be able to avoid two common errors which plague conversations. Sometimes, when we are unsure what to say, we may listen with half of our attention while we devote the other half to formulating a response. At other times we are so eager to communicate that we lapse into perfunctory listening while we wait to break in with our own comments. As good listeners, we will resist these impulses. We listen attentively and well so that, like Barnabas, we can encourage well.

3. Observing. Closely related to the skill of listening is the skill of observation. In this, too, Barnabas was practiced and skilled. When he arrived in Antioch, Luke reports, "he saw the evidence of the grace of God" (Acts 11:23). He had learned the art of careful observation and used this skill immediately and effectively upon his arrival.

In any conversation, the words themselves are only part of the communication process. Much of a speaker's meaning is communicated non-verbally with gestures, voice inflections, facial expressions, posture, emphasis, and tone of voice.

To listen well, we "listen" with our eyes as well as with our ears! We look directly into the speaker's eyes. We watch facial expression. We observe gestures. We take note of posture. All the while, we are aware of tone, inflection, and emphasis. We gather meaning from all of these sources in order to understand *all* that is being communicated, either intentionally or unintentionally.

At the same time, we are gathering information about the speaker from other sources. We take note of physical features, clothing, the decor and mood of the home or workplace, the condition of possessions, the demeanor of children, the person's interaction with spouse and peers, the literature he is reading. By observing such things, we will learn a great deal more about a speaker than words alone communicate.

4. Right living. Far more than any particular skills, Barnabas was a good encourager because he was a good man. His compassion, his sensitivity, his comfort, his timely challenges welled up, as it were, from within "a good man, full of the Holy Spirit and faith" (Acts 11:24).

Barnabas was respected and appreciated among the believers, Luke reports, because of his good character. He was credible. He had earned the trust of the believers; he had won the "right to be heard."

As encouragers, we will want (and need) to demonstrate this same kind of credibility in our character and lifestyle. It should be obvious to all that we are honest, even-handed, discreet (as in maintaining confidentiality), considerate, and respectful.

It is also vital for encouragers, like Barnabas, to be filled with the Holy Spirit. The Spirit can (and does) reveal unspoken thoughts, expose attitudes, and provide background information— supernaturally, through "promptings" or "inspirations" or, to be biblically precise, through words of knowledge and prophecy (Mark 2:8; Luke 19:5; John 4:17-18). In addition, the Spirit gives discernment into the source of difficulties, wisdom in applying biblical truth, and clarity in expressing concepts in the best way.

The third trait Luke attributes to Barnabas is faith, another primary asset of an encourager. Barnabas had a strong confidence in God based on Scripture and confirmed in his own experience.

From the Scriptures, he knew God's character. He also knew what God desires to do in and through people. With this knowledge informing his perspective, he was confident of what God could and would do in relation to any particular person.

From his own experience Barnabas gained the conviction from which he could speak forcefully and earnestly. In 2 Corinthians 1:3-4, Paul describes this dynamic: "Praise be to the God and Father of our Lord Jesus Christ, the Father of compassion and the God of all comfort, who comforts us in all our troubles, so that we can comfort those in any trouble with the comfort we ourselves have received from God." From the "comfort" he himself received—the word is *parakaleo*, encouragement—an encourager is able to comfort and encourage others. He is sure of it, he is convinced, because he is passing on the encouragement he himself has received.

"Who we are" is vitally important in encouragement. In fact, our encouragement is most often an expression of what we ourselves have learned and experienced. When we are a good person, full of the Holy Spirit and faith, we have a lot to give!

5. *Maintaining the vision.* It is noteworthy that Barnabas encouraged people with a clear and definite sense of purpose. He encouraged them "to remain true to the Lord with all their hearts" (Acts 11:23). Barnabas was not out to win friends and influence people. He was not seeking honor for himself. He was not building a constituency for eventual election to the apostolate. His sole aim was to encourage persons to remain true to the Lord as the highest and best aim of their lives.

An encourager remains true to this purpose by using biblical truth as the content of and basis of his encouragement. The Bible is the primary tool of the encourager. It is significant that Barnabas "met with the church and taught great numbers of people." The content of his encouragement was always biblical truth or, when he spoke from personal experience, based on biblical truth.

Barnabas, the master encourager, knew that the Scriptures provide the only adequate message for encouraging believers. He knew the Scriptures well, he held firmly to the trustworthy message, and shared it at every opportunity to encourage disciples in their walk with Christ.

6. *Recognizing potential.* Barnabas also had a knack for seeing the potential in people. He was able to discern strengths, perhaps even the strengths implicit in weaknesses, and visualize the development of these strengths after the teaching and empowering work of the Holy Spirit.

When he came to Antioch to give leadership to this emerging church, he saw an opportunity for the young Saul to develop his potential for preaching and teaching. He sought him out, gave him an invitation to serve with him, and brought him back to Antioch (Acts 11:25-26). Keenly aware of the potential in this young man, Barnabas took him on as an understudy and co-worker. "So for a whole year Barnabas and Saul met with the church and taught great numbers of people" (Acts 11:26).

As encouragers, desiring to do the same, we will look for potential in persons. We can develop the capacity to identify positive qualities, even ones that are latent in "negative" traits. Then we will anticipate the best, confidently expecting all of these qualities to be fully developed as the Holy Spirit refines the person's life and character. In anticipation of this, we can encourage participation in witness and service. Many times, we can facilitate this process by finding (or creating) opportunities for a person to utilize gifts and develop positive qualities. We will be eager to entrust persons with responsibility, sometimes before they are fully ready, because we are confident they will grow in the job. Even when an understudy surpasses us, as young Paul did Barnabas, we will be delighted. As an encouraging mentor, we will step aside to make room for an emerging worker and leader.

Perhaps better than anyone else in Scripture, Barnabas expresses the traits of an encourager. Those of us who contribute to the work of evangelism with the gift of encouragement do well to emulate him.

Encouragement—a ministry for all

In one sense, of course, the task of encouragement falls to the whole church. Some members, like Barnabas, have a special knack for encouragement. Yet all of us are instructed throughout the New Testament to encourage one another.

In many churches the pastor is responsible to discover who among the members is hurting or straying, and then to provide the encouragement that is needed. As a church grows, however, a pastor cannot keep up with the number of persons who need encouragement.

Some churches establish subgroupings within the congregation—Sunday school classes, love circles, care groups, Bible studies, home groups, cell groups, or whatever name they may be given. As such groups are organized, leaders have responsibility for the nurture and encouragement of participants. In this way congregations mobilize the whole church to encourage one another.

But even when pastors are active and the entire church is encouraging, there is still a need for special persons to encourage new converts. In the first three to six months of participation in church life, new converts are not yet integrated into the established web of caring relationships. They are—or, at least, still feel like—newcomers and, to differing degrees, outsiders.

These new converts need special attention during the interim between their initial participation and their full integration into the life of the congregation. Win Arn writes, "If these new members do not immediately develop meaningful friendship in their church, many of them will return to their old friendships—and ways—outside the church."[31] He suggests seven solid friendships as the norm for retaining new converts.

During this critical time, as part of the work of an evangelistic team, some persons will want to concentrate on encouraging these new converts. While others are working to help persons to become disciples, these persons are working to encourage—and *keep*—new converts.

The process of encouragement begins by going over the list of participants each week. The size of your church will determine whether you can manage the entire membership on one list, or whether you will need to consider separate lists for smaller groupings, such as departments or classes. Who was present? Who was missing? Why was this person absent? Is a pattern developing? Are we aware of particular stresses or strains? Is there any need for counsel or correction?

Once needs have been identified, they can be prioritized. Some persons will need immediate care. Others will benefit from a contact soon. Some can be kept in mind over a period of time.

The next step is to assign encouragers. In most instances, the one who knows the new convert best will be the best encourager. At other times, it is helpful to send a person who has experienced similar difficulties and overcome them. (See 2 Cor. 1:3-7.) Often, it is good to assign a team of persons with a blend of experiences—one who has overcome a similar problem, another who may be in the throes of the same struggle, and one who can provide biblical counsel for this particular difficulty.

For some persons, an invitation to our own home will be attractive. For others, conversation at a restaurant or coffee shop will be comfortable. Persons are often most at ease in their own home. Whenever possible, the persons should be contacted for an appointment to visit in their home or at some other convenient place.

In the conversation, we practice all the skills of encouragement. We listen attentively—with ears and eyes. We discern needs and potential. We determine whether to comfort or challenge. As appropriate, we offer biblical counsel and share confirming personal experiences. With the person's permission, we may pray.

In whatever ways it is done, the encouragement of new believers is vital in evangelism. Once the decision to follow Christ as Savior and Lord is made, the convert becomes a disciple who is committed to learning and living the teachings of Jesus. There will be notable, exhilarating successes. And there will be frustrating and discouraging failures. A life of discipleship is inevitably uneven; and in the ebb and flow of a developing Christian life, we all need encouragement. For the newest disciples, encouragement is not just helpful; it is crucial!

On Sundays when we sing the chorus, "I Have Decided to Follow Jesus," and I see tears slipping down Charlene's cheeks, I am reminded that her decision to turn back to Christ—and all the subsequent encouragement we provided—has wrought an incredible, dramatic, and joyous change in her life.

Whether in acute crisis, as Carl and Charlene were, or in slight "disrepair" as others have been, encouragement is vital for new disciples. When we are faithful in providing it, we insure that each of us, and all of us together, will be "built up until we all reach unity in the faith and in the knowledge of the Son of God and become mature, attaining to the whole measure of the fullness of Christ" (Eph. 4:12-13).

Activities

1. In the ebb and flow of a developing Christian life, we all need encouragement. Share from your own experience some of the times when you have needed encouragement. When have persons comforted you? When have you needed a challenge?

2. As you share these experiences with one another, practice the skills of good listening. Concentrate your full attention on the speaker. Listen for main ideas. Pay attention to facts supporting the main ideas. Watch facial expressions. Observe gestures. Take note of posture. Be aware of tone, inflection, and emphasis. Ask for clarification. Repeat the speaker's thought in your own words to be sure you understand correctly. When everyone has finished, take turns telling the story of another person, including both facts and feelings. When you finish, ask the original speaker to evaluate the accuracy and depth of your listening.

3. Practice your skill in seeing the strengths and potential in people. In a group of four to eight persons, write a short comment identifying a strength in every other person participating. All comments should be positive; you are practicing the identification of positive traits! When everyone is finished, name the first person to be described. Then have the rest of the group take turns sharing the strength they have written which pertains to the person. Continue this until each has heard what the others have written. As the exercise progresses, check your own assessments against the cumulative wisdom of the group. Have you been aware of the traits that are being identified?

4. Prepare an attendance record, listing all the participants in your church, class, or group. Now record participation for the current past week. Check with one or two other persons to be sure your record is correct. To the best of your knowledge, determine why each person was absent. Take note of persons who are sporadic in attendance. Identify ones who are struggling or hurting in some way. If possible, during your scheduled time for evangelism, arrange to meet with these persons in a suitable location to talk together. If that time is inconvenient, arrange to meet at another time or place. In the encounter, do your best to listen carefully and encourage helpfully.

9

Making It Happen

More than anyone else, one particular man has drawn me into the work of evangelism. Scores of pastors like me are involved in evangelism because of this man's efforts. New churches are being started across the continent because of his vision. Hundreds of persons are coming to the Lord in repentance and faith. Yet he is not an evangelist!

Bishop Don, as we called him, is an administrator. His expressed purpose in his first visit with us was to listen. Not knowing where to focus his attention as a bishop, he had asked the Lord, "What am I to do?" Now he was listening to his pastors and people as one way of hearing the Lord's response to his prayer question.

By the next year the Lord's answer was beginning to form in Bishop Don's mind. Persons were urging him to help small churches to grow. They were also cautioning him, "Don't start anything new!"

Toward that end, he began to study church growth at a nearby graduate school. Early on, he sensed that the Lord was calling him to mobilize the people in his area to support the existing churches and, in addition, to start new churches. Evidently, the Lord had vetoed the suggestion about not starting anything new!

If the other people were surprised at the audacity of his undertaking, my surprise came at a different point. I was surprised that Bishop Don was talking about evangelism! As I sized him up with my fresh-out-of seminary acumen, I noted that he had not distinguished himself in evangelism to this point in his ministry. I concluded that he was an unlikely person to lead churches into evangelism and church growth. So I watched with a blend of interest and skepticism as our unevangelistic bishop challenged his pastors and churches to grow.

Not much happened at first. Bishop Don cared for his various responsibilities. But all the while he was learning about church growth. As his understanding grew, he shared his insights and enthusiasm with his pastors and people. He identified an expert in the field, and persuaded the conference to hire him as a consultant.

Before long, Bishop Don had shaped a realistic plan to stimulate church growth by starting new churches in his conference. The project was approved and the money was budgeted. Incredibly, our unevangelistic bishop was ready to start his first church.

Bishop Don zeroed in on a pastor who had already started two thriving churches and persuaded him to accept an assignment as founding pastor of the new church. The first church was launched and grew into a sturdy congregation.

Meanwhile, Bishop Don was pressing ahead toward a second new church. Then he started a third and fourth, and so on at a pace roughly of one a year. While church planting pastors worked on site to build the new churches, Bishop Don quietly worked his successive miracles of persuasion and mobilization among the people of the established churches to generate enthusiasm, commitment, and funding.

Along with a growing number of proponents, there were numbers of critics. But Bishop Don, still big on communication, kept talking with everyone, for or against. He listened, learned, and responded. Sometimes he offered insights and assurances. Other times he altered a proposal or modified a timetable. Always he persisted in his determination to plant new churches.

As I continued to watch—from a safe distance—Bishop Don had some notable successes. Several existing churches began to grow. The first new church, once it caught its stride, grew to 200 persons.

At the same time, there were some glaring—and potentially demoralizing—failures. One church, after receiving thousands of dollars in funding, left the denomination without repaying the financial support it had received. One pastoral family fragmented and a new church shriveled. But Bishop Don kept going. It is a good thing, really, that his hair was thin before he ever started. He would surely have lost it in the process! As I watched him at conferences and meetings, he had an uncanny way of fulfilling all of his responsibilities. Yet his emphasis always came through most strongly for church growth. Most areas of church life, for example, he would delegate to capable lay leadership. But he was always present himself at planning sessions for evangelism and church growth. When budgets were presented, everything was adequately funded. But the money allotted for new churches was invariably the highest. When the conference decided to hire additional staff to assist Don, it was in the area of church growth.

After eight years of watching from the sidelines, my skepticism had melted away. Somehow, our unevangelistic Bishop Don had created a ground swell of commitment to church growth. He was guiding it to fruition in the establishment of new churches and the encouragement of existing ones. Bishop Don's ground swell crested into a wave of enthusiasm which swept over our whole denomination, catching up Connie and me up in the breathtaking ride we have been living in for the past eight years.

At first I could not comprehend how Bishop Don, without any evangelistic penchant that I could discern, was able to accomplish so much church growth. Now that I have been in the thick of evangelism myself for these eight years, I am able to see the secret of his effectiveness. Bishop Don may not have particular strengths in witnessing, proclamation, nurturing, and evangelistic prayer. But he has the ability to bring the gifts of many other persons together to make it happen. Bishop Don has the gift of leadership.

Evangelism proceeds in fits and starts when each person does his own thing. But when someone gives effective leadership, the gifts of many persons can be combined into an effective team that can reach multitudes of people. In evangelism the gift of leadership is indispensable!

In Romans 12, the Apostle Paul identifies leadership as one of the gifts of the Holy Spirit. In verse 8 he writes, "if [a person's gift] is leadership, let him govern diligently." The word translated here as "diligence" means with "haste" or "speed." By the enabling of the Holy Spirit, a leader has an ability for maintaining focus on goals to be achieved, monitoring progress toward these goals, and preventing people from being sidetracked in the pursuit of these goals. When someone is exercising this kind of leadership, persons can accomplish common goals in the least amount of time.

·In Titus 3:8 and 14, the Greek word translated "devote themselves" in the New International Version means literally to "stand before" or to "maintain." This word points out the need for perseverance in leadership. A leader cannot lose sight of essential purposes, activities, and results.

In 1 Timothy the Apostle Paul writes that one of the qualifications for overseers and deacons is to manage his family well. "Now the overseer . . . must manage his own family well and see that his children obey him with proper respect" (1 Tim. 3:2-4). Of deacons he writes, "A deacon . . . must manage his children and his household well" (1 Tim. 3:12). "Manage" is another of the New Testament's words for leadership, applied here to a father's role in the home and family. It suggests that the leader is to guide others toward a goal, in this case godly living and spiritual maturity, while living together in mutual love.

Just a few paragraphs later Paul applies this same word to leadership in the church. "The elders who direct the affairs of the church well are worthy of double honor, especially those whose work is preaching and teaching" (1 Tim. 5:17). As these elders direct the church, they give oversight and guidance which insures productive work and harmonious internal life.

In his letter to the Thessalonians, Paul uses still another word. "Now we ask you, brothers, to respect those who work hard among you, who are over you in the Lord and who admonish you" (1 Thess. 5:12). Paul's use of the word "over" implies responsibility for the Church. It suggests that the leader has been entrusted by Christ with the management of a particular part of his Church, and is accountable to him for the growth and maturation of this body. In this word the leader is a steward or manager, accountable to Jesus Christ, the head of the Church.

This same sense of accountability is repeated in Hebrews 13:17: "Obey your leaders and submit to their authority. They keep watch over you as men who must give an account. Obey them so that their work will be a joy, not a burden, for that would be of no advantage to you." The leader who operates in the authority bestowed by the church and confirmed by "the outcome of his life" (13:7) can expect cooperation and obedience from those who follow.

In this biblical word study we see that leadership is the ability: (1) to clearly articulate God's purpose for the future, (2) to communicate this objective in a way that keeps people focused on its attainment, (3) to mobilize and direct persons to work together harmoniously toward these goals, (4) to persevere despite setbacks, obstacles and digressions, and (5) to accomplish the goals for the glory of God.

As we gear up for evangelism as a cooperative effort in our own congregations, someone with these abilities is needed to give leadership to the common enterprise. Specifically, the leader will need to guide the group through four successive steps to "get things moving" in evangelism.

Determine to evangelize!

The first step is to determine to evangelize. A leader must be convinced, and then convince others, that evangelism is a primary task of the church. In a memorable analogy, Jesus compared himself to a grapevine. His disciples are the branches; his Father is the gardener or husbandman (John 15).

Jesus' emphasis throughout the analogy is on bearing fruit (vv. 2,4,5,8), culminating with the summation in verse 16, "I chose you to go and bear fruit—fruit that will last." The expectation of a healthy, well tended, grapevine is that it will bear fruit.

This is true of individual believers, and equally true of groups of believers. Our purpose as a congregation—our reason for existence—is to bear fruit. The consistent refrain in all the biblical analogies to the grapevine, whether applied individually or corporately, is that a healthy, well-tended vine *will* bear fruit.

We can think, with biblical precedent, of this fruit as "good works" which glorify God (Matt. 5:14-16; Eph. 2:10). We can consider fruit as the developing traits of a Christlike character (Gal. 6:22-23). We must also consider fruit, in its reproductive sense, to mean successful evangelism. A healthy, well-tended congregation, like the grapevine, will produce new disciples committed to Jesus Christ and his church.

That process begins when a group makes a firm commitment to evangelistic fruitfulness: we *will* bear fruit. Our aim, our purpose, our objective is to bear the fruit of lives converted and transformed through Jesus Christ. And we will measure our health and faithfulness by this criteria.

In some places this commitment will produce fruit easily. Growing conditions will be ideal and fruit will develop quickly. In other areas the evangelistic climate will be unfavorable and fruit may only develop slowly with painstaking work. But there is the potential for fruit anywhere because there are unchurched persons everywhere. A group of believers bears the responsibility to bear fruit in the place where it finds itself—or to expend itself trying. A leader's first step is to declare: we purpose to be fruitful here in this community, in this town, in this city—through this body of people!

Prune for growth

The second step is to focus a group's energies on a few key tasks. The leader must ask: among all the things that we are doing or might do, which ones make an effective contribution to evangelism and growth? Then he must direct the group's workforce in doing these things well.

Many churches resemble the luxuriant vine Jesus describes in John 15. To all appearances, the grapevine is strong and healthy. The plant is well watered. It is drawing a full complement of nutrients from the soil. It has the benefit of the bright sunlight. It is working hard to transform these resources of water, sun, and soil into growth. But all of the plant's energies are devoted to producing lush, green foliage. There is no fruit!

A vine needs to be tended by a vinedresser. The vinedresser knows which branches are potentially fruitful and which are not. He cuts away unproductive branches. He even cuts back potential fruitbearing branches. He prunes the vine radically and drastically because he wants the plant to do one thing well—to bear fruit.

A leader needs this same skill in the church. Like an untended grapevine, many churches appear strong and healthy.

They offer a full complement of services and activities. Volunteers are working to capacity—and beyond. Much is being done. But the church is not bearing the fruit of new believers! The church is only producing "branches and leaves."

The solution is not to add another program, one in evangelism. Rather, it is to skillfully prune away unproductive activities and services so that ones which are potentially fruitful can mature and produce. The responsibility of the one giving leadership in evangelism is to determine the essential functions which produce fruit, and to give direction in the process of pruning and reshaping all others.

With this concern in mind, I took stock of our own congregation. As a young congregation, just five years old at the time, we were concentrating on worship, nurture, and evangelism—or so I thought. I noted the emphasis in each of our meetings and discovered that we met once a week for worship, five times for nurture and fellowship, and not once for evangelism.

Unwittingly, I had been devoting a major portion of my time to activities which were essentially for fellowship. Our avowed purpose was to grow; yet without realizing it, we had drifted into a lopsided emphasis which was hindering growth.

Without telling anyone, I resolved to shift our emphasis to evangelism. I determined, first, that our most appealing meeting, apart from worship, would be for evangelism. To announce that I was downgrading any of our fellowship gatherings, I knew, would raise an outcry of dismay. So I said that in the interests of training, I would be encouraging others to share in giving the teachings in our nurture meetings. It was also time, I said, to involve other guitarists beside myself in the accompaniment of our choruses. We kept the same format and emphasis in these meetings, but the leadership was turned over to learners. In effect, I withdrew the "starting team" and put in our "second string." The "first string" was reassigned to developing first-rate music and teaching for our evangelistic meeting!

Within a couple of months, it was evident that my shift of emphasis was going to work. People continued to appreciate our nurture gatherings. But the evangelism group continued to grow until sixteen persons were regularly involved. (Previously, I had been fortunate to get one or two persons to go with me!) The music, the teaching, the sense of purpose and comraderie made this the most appealing event of the entire week. Within four months, RESCUE group meetings (short for *R*eaching, *E*quipping, *S*ending: *C*alling the *U*nchurched to *E*ternal Life) had become the place to be.

Without any drastic commotion or trauma, we had pruned away excess fellowship activities. Quietly, the emphasis shifted to evangelism. Now we are doing four things well—worship, nurture, fellowship, and evangelism. The components are right, the balance is right. We are doing just what we need to do to grow—and nothing more.

As we grow and mature as a congregation, we may be able to do additional things well. But our aim is to continually prune ourselves for optimum fruitfulness. We want our church body to be lean and trim, so that we will always have a competitive edge on Satan in the contest for unsaved and unchurched people!

The first step in pruning for growth is to locate a two-hour block of *prime* time for an evangelistic team to meet weekly. In the first hour team members can gather for training and inspiration. In the second they can scatter for the actual evangelistic work of prayer, witness, proclamation, encouragement, teaching, and behind-the-scenes support.

As you select the best time, you will need to consider two constituencies: the unchurched persons you want to reach and the workers you want to mobilize. When are the unchurched persons in your community home and accessible to your contacts? When can your workers be available? Many churches find that a week night works best. Some use Sunday afternoon. A few meet on Saturday mornings.

Once you have determined the best time, you will bump up against conflicting activities—and the pruning begins. How will you free up this time for evangelism? How can you release workers from other tasks? Something will have to go. What will it be?

Look at each of your scheduled activities. What is the primary emphasis of each? What is the balance among activities which feature worship, teaching, fellowship, evangelism, and service? The area which gets the most attention might benefit from some pruning. Or you may be overextended in all of these areas and need to reduce in all of them.

Though it is potentially disruptive, you may discontinue some activities. If interest is waning, you can let others die without taking any "heroic measures" to save them. Some can be de-emphasized. Others might be rescheduled. The pastor may need to give primary attention to a few key functions and delegate other responsibilities. Workers will need to be reassigned to new and different tasks. However you manage it, rearrange all your activities and workers around a priority for evangelism.

Believe me, pruning is hard! This spring I pruned several fruit trees in our backyard. Not having any experience at this, I needed to take the instructions in my gardening book by faith. Only with much hesitation and uneasiness was I able to cut away strong, healthy branches as the book directed. Numbers of times I agonized over a branch before I plunged ahead with my cutting and trimming.

Hard as that was, pruning a church is even harder! But it can be done. It must be done. The *only* way to bear fruit is to prune our church work and activities back to the point where we are doing a few things well.

Mobilize workers

Once you have a established a prime time and place for evangelism, you are ready for the third step: mobilizing workers. As we have seen, evangelism is the work of a team, with each worker contributing a gift into a blend that is productive in evangelism. Potential workers must be motivated to help; they must be trained in their particular tasks; and they must be guided in the accomplishment of their task.

The task of recruitment begins with prayer for workers. If a small group of persons is interested in evangelism, meet regularly to pray. Pray for workers among the congregation as a whole. Or pray through the church directory and, one by one, ask the Lord to send this person as a worker into his harvest field.

It is also important to talk with prospective workers. Without any pressure to enlist, communicate the vision of an evangelistic team which will meet regularly each week. Describe the diversity of opportunity, identifying gifts not normally associated with evangelism. As opportunities present themselves, share the vision with as many people as possible, particularly ones you sense may have a special calling to evangelism.

After you have taken time to pray and talk with people, ask the pastor to preach a "recruitment" message, culminating with an invitation to participate in evangelism. In advance of this message, send a letter of invitation to everyone in the congregation. Follow up with a kick-off dinner to solidify and confirm the commitments persons make following the message.

Once workers are committed to participation, the next task is training. One of the most intimidating things about evangelism is the fear of not knowing what to say or do in conversation with an unchurched person. With systematic, incremental training you can allay this fear, and prepare those workers who will eventually participate in evangelistic contacts.

The natural place to begin training in evangelism is with prayer, encouragement, and witnessing. Except for the newest converts, workers will be practiced in these. Evangelistic prayer and encouragement can be presented as a new application for already familiar practices. As presented in Chapter 4, witnessing is only a matter of sharing personal stories during conversations with unchurched persons. With this basic repertoire of skills, an evangelistic team can begin to function effectively.

In anticipation of persons who will respond, a trainer can introduce the proclamation of the gospel (Chapter 6). This usually stirs more apprehension. But careful teaching, blended with opportunities for demonstration, observation, and right-at-your-side support during initial applications of these skills, can lead most workers to proficiency in leading persons to pray to receive Christ.

In addition, workers can be trained to nurture converts in the basics of Christian living. Depending on the size of the response, you may want to prepare persons to teach groups of people in "new Christians" classes. Or you can train persons to work with new converts one-to-one over a period of weeks. The work of training never ends. As a worker learns and gains proficiency in a particular skill, that person in turn can train others. The more trained workers you have available, the more new workers you can train and the larger your team of workers, and the more persons will hear (and respond) to the good news about Jesus Christ. Training workers is vital!

As an expanding pool of trained workers becomes available, the next task is meaningful deployment. Fortunately, fulfilling work creates its own motivation. The best worker (and the best recruiter of new workers) is the one who is contributing in a meaningful way to a team effort that is producing "results" of conversions and church growth. An effective leader, therefore, will work hard to have meaningful, potentially productive assignments for each worker each week.

Finally, the task of mobilizing workers requires commendation and expressions of gratitude. Workers who are appreciated are enthusiastic and eager.

Oklahomans are big on football, so I have ample opportunity to follow the newspapers as enthusiasm mounts during the football season. I note the skill with which our successful Oklahoma coaches affirm their players. And I chuckle at the way our quarterbacks affirm their linemen; they are determined by their affirmation to keep their linemen motivated—and their own bodies intact.

Affirmation, in evangelism as in everything else, is an essential and vital part of the leadership job. In our congregation we keep statistics in order to measure and evaluate our progress—and to encourage our workers. We rarely cite statistics in our worship service to an entire congregation. But to our team we report on our progress and describe the advances we have made, even when they are only small ones. When workers see results and hear appreciation, they are encouraged and motivated for more.

Stick with it

A final responsibility of the one giving leadership in evangelism is to persevere. The leader bears the reponsibility to "go the distance" toward the objective of reaching persons for Jesus Christ. When others are wavering, the leader must demonstrate "stick-to-itiveness" and encourage others in their perseverance.

Again, the comparison to fruitfulness is an apt one. Fruit is the final result of an entire season of planting, watering, fertilizing, pruning, and tending. The gardener begins immediately after the previous growing season to prepare for the coming harvest. In the fall he prunes the tree and cultivates the soil. In the spring he adds nutrients. As the season develops he may spray his orchard for insects and pests. In severe weather he uses wind machines, sludge pots, or water sprays to protect the developing buds from freezing. At last the fruit ripens and the harvest begins. He has worked for a full year, without any fruit, in anticipation of this day.

Evangelism proceeds in the same way. First, leaders and team members must commit themselves to evangelism. Next they must prune in their congregational life for evangelistic effectiveness. Then they motivate and train people. Finally, they "hit their stride" and work in earnest with unchurched individuals and families. Initially so few people may respond that the numbers are "underwhelming."

Throughout this whole process, someone must have a tenacious, unshakable conviction that this work will eventuate in persons coming to Christ. Until the team has proven to itself that it can produce a credible harvest, the leader must believe for everyone. It may well be the leader's most demanding responsibility!

As one of the words describing leadership suggests, a leader must "stand before" the others. In the early days, before any tangible evidence is apparent, a leader must envision a developing evangelistic initiative and, beyond that, the initial converts and church members long before actual results appear.

For myself, I have battled to believe for evangelistic fruit. To work with diligence and joy during the time when there are no apparent results has been, to put it mildly, hard for me. Without any personal experience to guide and console us, our early mistakes and setbacks were utterly demoralizing. The first team I gathered "exploded" within three months. One of our workers experienced a relapse into alcoholism. Immediately she and her husband dropped out of our team and almost out of their marriage. Others began to quibble about methods and approaches. Within a few weeks the entire initiative had collapsed. It took me two years to pick myself up from that debacle and try again to rouse our people to intentional evangelism.

This requires more than a determination to "hang in there." If my own experience is any guide, I am convinced that a leader must deliberately and actively cultivate a perspective of faith and confidence.

That faith is grounded in the Word of God. Even when our experience does not warrant confidence, we can return to the truth of God's Word. Whether we are experiencing any results or not, Jesus has commanded us to go and make disciples; so we must. He has promised that when we pray according to his will, he will hear us and answer; so we keep praying. He has assured us that "he who goes out weeping, carrying seed to sow, will return with songs of joy, carrying his sheaves with him"; so despite our tears of fear and discouragement, we keep on sowing.

If confidence is based on our own abilities, that will be shaken and collapse. If we are motivated by the evangelistic responsiveness we perceive in our community, that will also prove inadequate. Leaders, if our hope rests in our workers, there will be times when they disappoint us. Team members, there may be days when the most determined leader is discouraged— perhaps to the point of despair. Ultimately, we together must build a tenacious confidence on the commands, instructions, and promises of Scripture related to evangelism.

There will be times when your church's evangelistic initiative seems to be faltering. Others in the congregation and participants on the team will be asking the question, "Is it working?" At every challenge you must ask a different question, "Is it true?" To answer, you must turn to the commands, the instructions, and the promises of God himself. These are the foundation of your faith.

In anticipation of these times, I have worked hard to build my counsel in each chapter on a firm biblical base. These biblical truths will hold you steady. There are more passages, of course, that give guidance for evangelism. You will likely find them while in the throes of discouragement and doubt—as I did. Discover them. Hang on to them. And on the basis of the promise and direction they give, press on!

A second important source of confidence is the personalized directives of the Holy Spirit. The Spirit will communicate with us directly at crucial times. He will impress us with Scripture passages which apply to us personally. When we encounter obstacles and setbacks, these personal directives from the Spirit can hold us steady.

Before we ever came to Oklahoma City, the Lord knew that the pressure of starting a new church would expose my wrong motivations and rub them raw. He anticipated that I would wake up to the bitter realization that I was here for the wrong reasons—and would want to quit in dismay and repentance. So, long before our first crisis, he assured me: "You did not choose me, but I chose you to go and bear fruit" (John 15:16).

Time and time again my naive aspirations gave way to disconcerting realities. My perspective would blur and my faith sag. But always I would return to this promise.

I understand now that the Spirit was reminding me: "I know all about your mixed motivations. I've known them from the beginning. Even so, I have chosen you. I have called you. You are doing this at my direction." The Spirit has given me this passage, I am sure, to hold me steady in that perspective. So I declare it as a prayer and a promise practically every day. Every time I do, I am renewed in my hope and faith.

The Spirit has given me other passages—Psalm 1, Joshua 1:5-9, and Ephesians 6:10-20. I hesitate to identify them, because yours will be different. The Spirit will quicken passages for you as a direct, personal word. Expect them. As they come, record them, memorize them, and declare them—day after day.

When the one giving leadership in evangelism actively cultivates a perspective of faith, he or she can communicate confidence to everyone on the team. When persons get sidetracked, the leader can redirect their energies back to productive work. When some workers "burn out," the leader can keep the team evangelizing. When persons criticize, the leader can listen and benefit from counsel that is helpful without being diverted from the task of evangelism; he or she can "keep the course" and hold the team steady. A leader can be tenacious in perseverance and draw others along by an unfailing commitment to press forward.

Leaders whose work is purposeful and productive have learned, first of all, to set a direction. They have the courage and wisdom to prune for fruitfulness so that the congregation can do a few things well. They actively work to mobilize, train, and deploy workers. And they are tenacious in their faith that their church will bear fruit.

These four ingredients spell the difference between a church that is "running in place" and one that is "moving forward." The tendency for any congregation, whether a new or existing one, is to continue "as is." Most churches continue year after year with the same people, the same basic activities, the same approximate attendance. Everyone works hard and well. But there is little growth and development.

Opposed to this is a congregation that benefits from leadership that gets things moving with actual advances in workers, evangelistic skills, attendance, membership, and maturity. Leaders who give a group of people clear objectives and dynamic direction is not just making the machinery run. They can actually get the machine to move forward!

It is a demanding task, a great responsibility. When we catch the vision for teamwork in evangelism, it is indispensable. You may have never personally "won" anyone to the Lord, but if your ability is to give leadership, that may be just what your congregation needs to get moving in this vital area of church life and growth.

Activities

1. Think of the good leaders with whom you have worked. What were characteristic traits? What strengths enabled these persons to give good leadership? Compare your observations with the responsibilities of a leader identified in the biblical word study of leadership.

2. One responsibility of a leader in evangelism is to convince others that evangelism is a primary task of the church. What does your church say are its priorities? Now examine the function of individual services and activities. Note the deployment of workers. Based on the use of time, money, and people, what are your group's actual priorities? Are these the priorities you want to have?

3. A helpful approach in giving evangelism priority is to assign the best possible time to evangelism. Assume for a moment that there were no conflicting services and activities. At what time would potential workers be able to participate most easily? At what times are unchurched persons most readily available for telephone calls and visits? Assume now that you can use a two-hour block of this prime time for evangelism. What possible changes and rearrangements would make this possible?

As you have read this book and practiced the activities, you have developed a repertoire of evangelistic skills.

Perhaps you already have been putting these skills into actual use—either on your own, in your study group, or as a part of a larger program of evangelism in your congregation.

If not, you are ready to begin weekly evangelistic contacts. Work in conjunction with your pastor and select someone (at least on a temporary basis) to provide coordination. (Worksheet 15 outlines the responsibilities our congregation has given to our evangelistic team leader. You may need to adapt this to your own situation.)

Assign some persons to schedule appointments. Give others assignments in prayer. Send some out to encourage new persons currently participating in your congregation. Deploy others to visit unchurched persons—to become acquainted, share church and personal testimonies, extend an invitation to your church and, when appropriate, to pray. (See Worksheets 12 and 13, pp. 231-233.)

Allow persons to express preferences in accepting assignments. At the same time, encourage persons to try different assignments in the remaining weeks of this study. Use Worksheet 14 (p. 234) to record these assignments. (The next chapter outlines a variety of additional responsibilities that will need to be assigned in the coming weeks as your evangelism program moves from practice in the classroom to reality in your community.)

10

Behind the Scenes

"Hi, Jamie!" With this greeting, two more people entered the home. Conversation was animated, with Jamie's voice rising above the others. At seven o'clock the group began to sing, "Freely, freely you have received; freely, freely give. Go in my name and because you believe, others will know that I live."

After a prayer of praise and dedication, the leader distributed an outline of the teaching for the evening. He introduced a particular aspect of the evangelistic task, highlighted key biblical passages, and illustrated from personal experience. Several questions were asked and comments of assent were given. By the time he finished, the group had gained more insights into evangelism and outreach.

After a brief exchange of questions to clarify assignments and travel directions, the group paused for another prayer. Then, still talking volubly, groups of two and three left for their assignments. In a few moments, all had left . . . except Jamie.

As other team members dispersed for their assignments, Jamie sat down at her typewriter to do hers: typing letters to the guests who had come to church the past Sunday, and to persons with whom we had scheduled an appointment for the following week. With that finished, she addressed postcards inviting "fringe" persons to a picnic the following Sunday.

As the survey teams returned to the home, they handed Jamie the names and addresses of seven newly discovered unchurched families. For the moment Jamie laid them aside. Before mailtime the next day she would have handwritten letters of appreciation to each family, enclosed a brochure describing our church, and mailed them. Right now, she had another opportunity as she sat at the kitchen table with an evangelistic worker who had returned from her assignment—to talk and to encourage.

At first it seems like Jamie is left out of the action. In reality she is doing more than her share! But you have to look closely, because everything that Jamie does is behind the scenes. Week after week, she faithfully does the hidden tasks that keep our evangelistic team functioning without disruption.

The work of evangelism advances with a few great evangelists and an eager corps of lay witnesses, encouragers, and teachers. But behind the scenes there are many more who work faithfully and quietly to support the ongoing task of evangelization.

We often think that this is a modern phenomenon. When we read about the work of evangelism in the New Testament, it is tempting to visualize a great enterprise which proceeded without mundane chores and small tasks. The stirring messages and extraordinary miracles of the apostles by themselves, we think, culminated in new churches springing up rapidly throughout the Roman Empire.

By comparison, our efforts in evangelism seem to get bogged down in the details of pamphlets, tracts, mailing lists, chairs, overhead projectors, and letters. We sometimes feel we have diminished a great undertaking with a mountain of minutia.

But look again at the New Testament. Commonplace chores and mundane tasks were as much a part of the evangelistic enterprise then as they are today. Scattered throughout the New Testament are references to people who worked behind the scenes to assist and support the apostles and missionary teams in their evangelistic endeavors.

We are familiar with the names of Peter, Paul, Barnabas, Timothy, Apollos, and Silas. But when we look more closely at the biblical account, we meet a host of other persons with more or less unfamiliar names like Mary, Simon, Lydia, Aquilla and Priscilla, Luke, Tertius, Gaius, Sosthenes, Stephanas, Fortunatus, Achaicus, Tychicus, Epaphroditus, Onesimus, Aristarchus, and Demas. Apart from their quiet contributions, the work of evangelism would have been sharply diminished and perceptibly slowed.

What did they do?

Many provided hospitality. Mary opened her home to an emergency prayer meeting when Peter was imprisoned by Herod (Acts 12:12). Simon the tanner offered overnight hospitality to Peter when he was in Joppa (Acts 10:6). Lydia insisted that Paul and his companions accept her hospitality during their stay in Philippi (Acts 16:15, 40).

Aquila and Priscilla offered hospitality to the Apostle Paul—and a tentmaking job as well (Acts 18:3). When this couple heard Apollos speaking accurately but incompletely about Jesus, "they invited him to their home and explained to him the way of God more adequately" (Acts 18:26). They also welcomed a church into their home to meet regularly for worship (Rom. 16:3-5; 1 Cor. 16:19).

Gaius extended hospitality to the Apostle Paul along with other itinerant evangelists and prophets and also to a church that met in his home (Rom. 16:23; 3 John 1:5-8). Nympha opened her home as a meeting place for a church, as did Archippus (Col. 4:15; Philem. 2). Paul asked Philemon to prepare a guest room for him in preparation for a time when he would accept his hospitality (Philem. 22).

Evangelism in the New Testament also involved much writing. The apostles corresponded extensively with churches, co-workers, and individual believers. Since writing was a specialized skill at the time, the normal custom was to dictate a letter to an amanuensis, or secretary, who would write the message word for word on parchment. Tertius assisted Paul as a writer for the book of Romans (Rom. 16:22). Sosthenes was the apostle's secretary for 1 Corinthians (1 Cor. 1:1).

At times an amanuensis assisted in composing a letter in the way that a co-author or editor "fleshes out" the material of writers today. The way Paul began several of his letters suggests that some of his co-workers may have assisted him as writers. As partners in ministry and evangelists in their own right, Paul may have given these men great freedom in the composition of the letter. Timothy may have assisted Paul in this way with 2 Corinthians, Philippians, and Colossians (2 Cor. 1:1; Phil. 1:1; Col. 1:1). Together, Silas and Timothy may have assisted Paul with his letters to the Thessalonians (1 Thess. 1:1; 2 Thess. 1:1). It seems probable that Peter, with a limited knowledge of literary Greek, may have given Silvanus (Silas, who had been Paul's co-worker for several years) an outline of the content, allowed him the freedom to compose the wording, and then added a conclusion in his own hand (1 Peter 5:12-14).

The highest level of writing is that of the writers of the gospels. All four gospels present the historical facts about Jesus. But each writer presents the life and teaching of Jesus in a different manner for a different audience. Matthew wrote to convince Jewish readers that Jesus is their royal Messiah. Mark described the events of Jesus' life to Gentile readers, and probably for the Romans in particular. Luke was written to attract and to win to the Christian faith cultured Greek readers, like Theophilus, to whom the book is dedicated. John was probably the last of the gospels to be written. It supplements the earlier books by Matthew, Mark, and Luke with additional historical data, particularly of Jesus' ministry in Judea, and in a simple yet profound way emphasizes Jesus as the climax of God's self-revelation.

Each gospel writer selected material for use from a great quantity of possible information (John 21:25). Each presented the information accurately. But the language and style differ. The emphases are different. The details which they include vary, as do the sequences of certain events. In each account the writer emphasized what he felt was most valuable for the special reading public he had in mind. Therefore, he chose materials, accounts, and teachings which were most suitable to accomplish his purpose.

The writers are evangelists in their own right. With a high degree of insight and sensitivity, they are presenting the good news about Jesus to a particular readership in order to persuade them to accept the good news that Jesus Christ is Savior and Lord.[32]

Another task related to letter-writing was messenger services. At that time there was no organized system for carrying and delivering private letters. The only postal service in the Roman Empire was reserved almost exclusively for official correspondence. Private letter writers had to rely on special messengers or friendly travelers to carry their letters to their destination.[33]

Paul used several persons that we know of to deliver his

letters. Tychicus carried the letters to the Ephesians and Colossians (Eph. 6:21; Col. 4:7-8). The letter to the Philippians was carried to the church by Epaphroditus, who earlier had carried a financial gift to Paul (Phil. 2:25-30; 4:18). The personal letter to Philemon was carried, we can surmise from the context, by Onesimus (Philem. 8-21). The couriers for the other letters are not identified, but we can assume that for each letter someone served the cause of evangelism in this practical, supportive way.

Some persons served behind the scenes with specialized skills. Luke may have assisted Paul in evangelism, as his writing in Luke and Acts demonstrates he was well able to do. But it is also likely that he served Paul as a sort of personal physician (Col. 4:14.) Certainly, there are a number of indications in Paul's writings that he could have benefitted from the services of a physician (2 Cor. 12:7-8; Gal. 4:13-15; 6:11).

Some persons seem to have served Paul as personal aides, doing any number of small tasks to assist the apostle in his ongoing evangelistic work. Epaphroditus was sent by the church at Philippi as a courier with a gift of money—and to render his personal services as well. Paul wrote of Epaphroditus as "your messenger, whom you sent to take care of my needs." The Corinthian church may have given three men a task similar to that of Epaphroditus's. Paul wrote, "I was glad when Stephanas, Fortunatus and Achaicus arrived, because they have supplied what was lacking from you" (1 Cor. 16:17).

In addition to these tasks, numbers of persons contributed to the team effort in ways that are not identified. At the head of his final greetings in his letter to the Romans, Paul introduced Phoebe, traveling to Rome soon, as "a servant of the church of Cenchrea," who has been "a great help to many people, including me" (Rom. 16:1-2). In the same list of greetings, he saluted "Mary, who worked very hard for you" (Rom. 16:6). He greeted Urbanus as "a fellow worker in Christ" (16:9).

In Colossians Paul named Aristarchus, Mark, and Jesus (called Justus) as "fellow workers" (Col. 4:10-11). We can also assume that Epaphras, Luke, and Demas were working with him at the time (Col. 4:12-14).

In his second letter to Timothy, Paul identified Erastus and Trophimus as persons who were (or had been) working with him in evangelism. Writing to Titus, Paul indicated that he would send Artemas or Tychicus, presumably to assist Titus in his evangelistic work (Titus 3:12). In greeting Philemon in his letter, Paul referred to him as a "dear friend and fellow worker" (Philem. 1). In his concluding greetings, he listed Mark, Aristarchus, Demas and Luke as "fellow workers."

Paul did not identify the particular services of these individuals. But because they had been a help to him in his work, which was primarily evangelism, we can assume that, however large or small their unidentified contributions, they were contributing to the ongoing work of evangelism.

Thus we see that the New Testament is filled with persons actively involved in the work of evangelism. A few are familiar to us as apostles and evangelists. Some were associates or understudies, working as preachers, teachers, prophets and pastors in direct evangelism. Clearly, a number of others contributed to the ongoing work of evangelism in what we might call "support services"— as secretaries, editorial assistants, writers, hosts and hostesses, and administrative and personal aides.

These same gifts and contributions are needed now. This is true on a large scale for the crusades of evangelists such as Billy Graham, Leighton Ford, Luis Palau, and others. It is equally true for the traveling teams in the Cursillo movement among Roman Catholics, the lay witness movement among the Methodists, and the revival movement among evangelicals. But since most of us will contribute to the evangelistic endeavors of a local church and all of us—even ones with itinerant ministries—will get our initial experience in our home church or college Christian fellowship, I will concentrate on application in these settings. What are some of the ways we can assist the work of evangelism behind the scenes in our own congregation?

Hospitality

Like Gaius, we will have opportunities to offer hospitality which serves the cause of evangelism. The most obvious parallel is to provide accommodations for evangelistic workers who travel to work with our congregation. Your church may bring in an evangelist for a series of special services. Increasingly, churches are turning to church growth consultants for advice and counsel. At times a team of workers may come from another congregation to assist in a special short-term project to contact hundreds of homes with flyers, door-to-door surveys, or some other team effort. Unless these persons request commercial accommodations, which are more expensive, they will need hospitality.

Another way to contribute to evangelism with hospitality is to invite persons to meals, desserts, or recreational activities. Meals are a great way to build a friendship—and there are all kinds of variations on this theme. In the summer, you might invite persons to a backyard barbeque or to make some home-made ice cream. If you have some special attraction—like a pool, trampoline, or croquet-smooth lawn—you can enjoy recreation and a snack. You can get together with another person for lunch at a nearby restaurant or coffee shop. Two couples can go out together for a meal and entertainment. A baseball game, bowling, or miniature golf can provide a relaxed and mutually enjoyable setting for building friendships.

When your church is successful at finding and winning unchurched persons, the early development of friendship is indispensable. Your availability to offer hospitality to these persons can "make" or "break" their participation in your church.

One of the most immediate and regular contributions you can make in the area of hospitality is in childcare. When a parent is able to participate in a concerted evangelistic initiative only when children are well cared for, childcare becomes a contribution to evangelism.

In our church we have offered everyone the opportunity to work in evangelism. To fulfill this pledge, we have had to be creative in working with a variety of home circumstances, especially those of our single parents. One of our parents has arranged for a relative to care for her children on the evenings we meet for evangelistic work. For another we have asked two of our teenagers to care for her daughters—as their contribution to evangelism.

Writing

As it was in the New Testament, writing is also an essential contribution to our evangelistic efforts. Written materials cannot substitute for personal interaction, but they do furnish valuable assistance in communication. And the ones who develop them are an integral part of an evangelistic team.

At the highest level, persons who communicate well in writing are needed to articulate "who we are." In our increasingly pluralistic society, the problem of identity is an acute one. This is true even when a church has a well-known denominational identity, with the unchurched population having at least an impression of the denomination's principle beliefs and practices. But even within well-known denominations, the "personality" of individual congregations will vary and this will need to be communicated.

For smaller demoninations and for new congregations— especially in an area where the larger group is not well known— the problem of identity is acute. In a time when cults and quasi-Christian groups are active in proselyting, people want to know "who we are." Even when we are not mistaken for these groups, persons want to "check out" a church's teachings, practices, services, and community life before they take any further steps toward involvement.

We communicate our identity in personal conversations and even more by the way we live before friends and neighbors. But full, precise communication to unchurched persons often requires written pieces that are attractive, clear, and understandable.

A church (or denomination) which is committed to evangelism will provide "identity" literature in a variety of forms, and a local congregation will be wise to take full advantage of these. But in our experience these denominational pieces are not enough. We have needed materials which address the specific needs of our community. So we have developed materials of our own.

One easy means has been to adapt articles and brochures already available. In one case we adapted a brochure developed by our mission board to recruit mission workers. The title, "Isn't it time we got to know each other?" was catchy—and fit our need as an "unknown" church here in Oklahoma City. With permission, we rewrote the script slightly, imprinted our church name, added a schedule of our services and reprinted the brochure as our own. It has been one of our most useful identity pieces.

At other times we utilize articles in our denominational

magazine, particularly ones written by persons in our congregation. When one of our men described the growth in the early years of our congregation in an article entitled "People told people—church planting in Oklahoma City," we secured permission to use the article, verbatim, in a recruitment brochure we developed for our evangelism initiatives. By adapting the magazine's own artwork and adding the specific opportunities for witness, we have an attractive and compelling invitation to participate in evangelism—with very little work.

We have also watched for articles in our denomination's scholarly journal. Most articles are written in academic style. But among them I discovered an interpretive essay describing the essence of our denomination, written in a popular style. We prepared a title page, and reprinted it with permission as a small booklet as one more way to clearly and persuasively describe ourselves to our community.

We have also designed our newsletter to communicate our identity. We determined that our newsletter, which we mail to a constituency almost five times the size of our normal Sunday worship attendance, will not be a sloppy, mimeographed collection of church news. Ours is designed in both style and format to look like a brochure. The first page is an identity piece. In a sharp, clear, succinct way we highlight one aspect of "who we are." At the suggestion of one of our newest members, we include testimonies (often with pictures which accomplish the same purpose) with a personal narrative. Our appeal in this first page is to all the unchurched persons who are receiving our newsletter. It is one more way to communicate who we are to persons who are considering us as a church home.

In addition, we have blended a number of these identity statements and testimonies into a brochure which we hand to guests who are worshipping with us for the first time. In place of the "in group" information which fills the typical bulletin, this brochure describes who we are with short, clear statements, testimonies, and a basic orientation to our worship service, Sunday school, services, and activities. The artwork and layout is attractive. It includes pictures. All together, it introduces our congregation to the first-timer who may be ill at ease and full of questions in a new and unfamiliar setting.

All of this can be incorporated into the work of an evangelism team. As others are telephoning and visiting, a "print team" can do its evangelistic work of writing, editing, designing, and typing. Someone may be interviewing a new believer or church worker—in order to develop a testimony. Another may be paging through church magazines for artwork (to be used after securing permissions). One may be writing a new identity piece. Another may be typing or editing.

This vital part of our evangelistic work is not left undone, or done hastily by an overworked staff. It is done, in increments—week after week—by persons with interest and aptitude in writing and promotion. It is one more way for persons with specialized skills, not normally associated with evangelism, to participate joyfully and productively in the great work of telling the good news—in print!

Secretarial work

Another major behind-the-scenes contribution is secretarial and clerical work. Like the early church secretaries Tertius and Sosthenes, someone must type the letters. Like Tychicus and Epaphroditus, others must see that they arrive at their destination. And like Onesiphorus, some help in many unnamed ways.

In our evangelistic contacts, we generally telephone to set up an appointment, then send a letter confirming the purpose of our visit and the time we plan to arrive. As many churches do, we respond to guests in our worship services with a letter. Often we will contact absentees and irregular attenders with a postcard or letter. We do our best to communicate at appropriate intervals with our prayer partners. We send a letter of appreciation, with a brochure describing our church, to persons who have responded to the questions on our door-to-door survey. Some persons work as part of our evangelism team by typing and writing these letters.

Our secretarial workers also handle our mailings. Each month they process our newsletter, preparing them in the meticulous manner required for bulk mailings. When we have special events designed especially to attract unchurched friends and neighbors to our church, they prepare postcard announcements.

While we keep records of the total number of persons at our services and activities, the more important records for our evangelism team is the weekly report on individual persons. Who attended our worship service? Who stayed for Sunday school? Were any of the family absent? Is this person's attendance consistent or irregular? This information is invaluable for the one who makes assignments each week for our evangelistic team. When we know who is missing—and can discover why—we can deploy our encouragers accordingly. When we can identify the first-timers, we can respond immediately with supportive contacts. So one clerical responsibility is to provide a current, person-by-person report on attendance—available in a concise form to our evangelistic team.

We also compile a list of the persons the team has contacted, the dates of the contact, and brief notations of the results of the contact. In subsequent contacts, we build on the information gained in our initial conversations. Then we cross reference our evangelistic contacts with our attendance reports to determine how we are doing!

When we evaluate the work of our team, it is also important to know how many times we have shared the gospel, how many persons have prayed to receive Christ, how many evangelistic visits, and how many encouragement visits were made, and how many persons have participated week by week on our evangelistic team. So we keep records of these statistics.

When we canvass a neighborhood with door-to-door surveys, we keep the survey sheets for future analysis. We keep the guest cards filled out by persons visiting our church for the first time. And we keep a back file of newcomer listings, for occasional reference to a person who was contacted some time earlier.

From these various records, we compile mailing lists. Persons who were surveyed and who gave their consent for us to "stay in touch" are transferred to the mailing list for our monthly newsletter. We maintain a mailing list for our prayer partners so we can communicate prayer requests and answers to prayer.

Our clerical workers also maintain a storeroom of materials we use for evangelism—brochures, testimony tracts, identity pieces, handouts for new Christians classes, Bible studies and expanded outlines. When the supply of these gets low, they order or photocopy more.

Quietly, sometimes laboriously, clerical workers gather, file, and systematize basic information that guides evangelism. In their clerical work they collect and collate the raw data which allows a team to "feel the pulse" of the spiritual body to whose growth they are committed. They supply statistics for motivation and encouragement. They "break them down" into individual persons, in definite places, with particular needs—so that the team can deploy its various skills and experiences most effectively. They keep communication flowing to prayer partners so fervent prayers keep rising toward heaven. They turn a prospect into a real person—with a name, residence, and telephone number. Praise God for these behind-the-scenes workers!

Specialized skills

The final worker behind the scenes is one who specializes in one or more miscellaneous chores—tasks that contribute to our evangelistic outreach, directly or indirectly, and should be done . . . but never seem to be accomplished because a pastor or church staff does not have time.

As a new church, meeting in an unadorned and nondescript multi-purpose room—with cement block walls, folding dividers, streaked windows and scuffed tile floors—we made a special effort to transform our meeting place into a worshipful setting. We succeeded to a remarkable degree because persons were willing to make a banner, purchase plants, build a pulpit/storage cabinet, and arrange for chairs to be set up (and taken down) weekly. All of this required innumerable telephone calls, supply trips, thank you letters, reminders, and "petty cash" money—in short, a multitude of miscellaneous tasks. But, as persons came forward to guide these projects into reality, our "sanctuary" has been transformed. Now we invite persons to worship with us without any fears that the setting will detract from their worship and fellowship. All because some cared about the small details and saw these special projects through to completion.

A similar project which has contributed to the appeal of our worship services for first-time guests is a chorus book. Many unchurched persons are unfamiliar with the hymns in our hymnbook and even with the hymnic style. We have responded to this need with Scripture choruses, accompanied by guitars. The choruses we were using and wanted to use are only available in a number of different songbooks, so we decided to create our own songbook. Over the span of a couple of years, several persons selected the songs, wrote to publishers for copyright permissions, composed the correct attributions, prepared the photo-ready copy, and personally did all the photocopying and stapling. Thanks to their perseverance in this multitude of small tasks, we now have an attractive and useful chorus book that we feel makes our worship more attractive and enjoyable for everyone, and particularly for the newcomers among us.

One summer Dave, one of our laymen, spent time scouting for the best location for a second church here in Oklahoma City. As we will see in Chapter 12, it is possible to identify particular groups of unchurched people, some of whom, even in our own communities, are not being effectively evangelized. Often, to identify and locate these groups of people takes extensive legwork and becomes a specialized task. Dave is a school counselor by profession, and has not had specialized training in preliminary research for evangelistic initiatives. But with the guidance of a church growth consultant, he has been able to identify areas which, at this time, seem most suitable for another church planting initiative in Oklahoma City.

Another way that persons can use specialized skills in a supportive role is to prepare accurate statistical "pictures" of a church's growth or decline. For many of us, statistical records, calculations, and graphs are tedious and onerous work. But for others there is special delight in minute statistical analysis. Before he moved away in a job transfer, one of our members took special joy in this task. He described himself as a "gnome" working happily, off by himself, at his statistical chores. Monthly he would update his graphs and, on the basis of his analysis, provide a running commentary on our progress for me. At our annual council meeting, Loren would present his graph along with a written analysis for the congregation. His insights and observations often encouraged us and kept us on track in our evangelistic initiatives. Consistently, we have had a clear picture of our progress—and at times, lack of it—and were able to learn from our mistakes quickly because Loren, our behind-the-scenes gnome, cared enough to contribute to our evangelistic endeavors in this special and helpful way.

Such careful and thorough analysis can assist your church toward a long-range perspective. To do this well, it is advisable to keep statistics in a manner taught by the proponents of church growth. One of the best instruction books for this is Bob Waymire and C. Peter Wagner's *The Church Growth Survey Handbook*.[34] Using the methodology in this handbook, even a novice statistician can determine annual growth rates (AGR) and decadal growth rates (DGR) for your church. An industrious analyst can prepare a comprehensive study complete with a community analysis, a brief history of your church, a description and diagnosis of growth patterns, and a five-year growth projection.

Any of these jobs left undone are a drag on the effectiveness of an evangelistic team. When persons gifted in personal witness or intercession, for example, are diverted to these tasks, their progress is slowed. But when persons are ready and willing to quietly and conscientiously work behind the scenes in innumerable small ways, their modest and varied contributions add up to an enormous boost for the overall effectiveness of an evangelistic team. It is an honored responsibility! The Apostle Paul urges recognition for Epaphroditus, one of his behind-the-scenes workers: "Welcome him in the Lord with great joy, and honor men like him" (Phil. 2:29). And he says of Stephanas and his household who devoted themselves to helpful service, "Such men deserve recognition" (1 Cor. 16:15,18).

Activities

1. The work of evangelism advances with a few great evangelists and an eager corps of lay witnesses, encouragers, and teachers. Behind the scenes there are many more who work faithfully and quietly to support the ongoing task of evangelization. How many of the support tasks can you identify in the evangelistic initiatives at your church? If you are just developing an initiative, which ones will you need?

2. One way to contribute to evangelism is to invite persons to meals, desserts, or recreational activities. Talk about ways you can "stir up" one another to use these means to build friendships for the sake of evangelism or encouragement.

3. Develop a personal testimony brochure for possible use by your evangelism team. Type your personal testimony or that of someone else in your church (written in session five) in three columns on an 8 1/2" by 11" sheet of paper, turned sideways. Then take another sheet of paper, also folded in thirds, and in the panel to the right place a title, along with any black and white artwork which conveys the theme of the testimony. Now photocopy the testimony brochure.

4. Gather the statistics you need to develop a profile of your church's growth over the past five to ten years. On a line graph, chart average worship attendance, Sunday school attendance and membership. In addition, calculate an average of these three statistics for a composite statistic. For a more comprehensive analysis (as a special project), use the methodology in Bob Waymire and C. Peter Wagner's *The Church Growth Survey Handbook* (see footnote 34).

11

If You Love One Another

"Hi! How are you this morning?" As our people gathered for worship, Ira moved among them, greeting each one by name. He would introduce himself to guests and concentrate on learning their names. He never seemed hurried. Yet he would talk with everyone—greeting, listening, encouraging, laughing.

Throughout the morning he pitched in wherever he was needed. Months before, he had stepped out of Sunday school teaching to give our "new blood" a chance. Now he sat in on the class of one of our newest adult teachers. He would ask questions or make comments designed to elicit a response, quietly helping the new teacher to focus discussion on a pertinent point or issue. When our service was over, he was among the first to begin stacking chairs, as we always need to do in our rented facility.

As Ira worked, I thought back to our earliest days as a church. At that time I marveled that a man of such stature would work with me in even the smallest tasks. He had earned his Ph.D. degree from Oklahoma University. He had been president of a Bible school and superintendent of a public school district. His net worth was well beyond that of anyone else in our young church. Yet he had made himself readily available for *anything* that needed to be done.

When I first began door-to-door canvassing, Ira went with me. When we needed an adult Sunday school teacher, Ira taught in an outstanding manner. When our young church needed a youth leader, no one else was able to manage this tough group of kids. So at the age of 62, Ira took them on! He struggled to make biblical truth interesting and relevant to their unusual needs. Even though he was not an outdoors person, he organized (and

161

led) water-skiing excursions, camping trips, and canoeing trips for the young people.

Ira accepted leadership positions until others were ready to assume these responsibilities. Then he stepped out of them as easily as he stepped in, always eager for others to move into leadership. His contribution was always supportive and constructive, never obstructive or reactionary. In all of this he worked hard. While others called for action, Ira took action. As chairman of our land search committee, he put in hours and hours of legwork tracking down leads, poring over courthouse records, and contacting property owners. As treasurer, he and his wife kept an accurate accounting of our financial resources and complete records of donors and designations. Each year he would write a personal letter to each contributor, indicating the amount given and adding a personal word of appreciation.

More striking than any of this was his care for our people. In conversations he listened for clues that indicated a person was troubled or struggling. Whenever he could, he would respond with practical help. One of our teenagers needed to interview an "older person" for a school assignment, and Ira offered to be his interviewee. One family was considering purchasing a home and, at their request, Ira gave counsel. Two families became estranged, and Ira guided them toward reconciliation. Another needed a car, and Ira loaned them one of his, the better one.

With more perception than any of us, Ira understood that the evangelization of a new convert requires a thriving Christian environment. He knew that the Holy Spirit does not place spiritual "babies" in nurseries that are destructive to their health and development. He entrusts them to churches which will provide a healthy, constructive environment with attitudes and actions that are actively supportive of new converts.

Luke describes such an environment in the early church: "They devoted themselves to the apostles' teaching and to the fellowship, to the breaking of bread and to prayer. Everyone was filled with awe, and many wonders and miraculous signs were done by the apostles. All the believers were together and had everything in common. Selling their possessions and goods, they gave to anyone as he had need. Every day they continued to meet together in the temple courts. They broke bread in their homes and ate together with glad and sincere hearts, praising God and enjoying the favor of all the people. And the Lord added to their number daily those who were being saved" (Acts 2:42-47). The apostles were actively continuing Jesus' work of teaching, preaching and healing (vv. 42-43). The early church was demonstrating the realities that the apostles were proclaiming. And the evangelistic impact was astounding!

Proclamation and demonstration! This combination is unbeatable in our individual initiatives. It is equally vital for all of us together, in community. When seekers or converts come among us for the first time, they hear what we say—and they feel who we are. In the early weeks of their participation, new persons sense the realities of righteousness, peace and joy, and are bonded to us. Or they feel the lack of them, and draw back.

The apostles recognized the crucial importance of this kind of community life. In a variety of "one another" passages scattered throughout the New Testament, they urge believers to concentrate on the quality of their interaction. These passages (the actual wording taken from various translations) describe the attitudes and actions which create a healthy, supportive environment for everyone in the church:

Statement	Reference
Love one another	John 13:34-35
Be devoted to one another; give preference to one another	Romans 12:10
Be of same mind toward one another	Romans 12:16
Love one another	Romans 13:8
Let us not judge one another	Romans 14:13
Pursue the things that make for the building up of one another	Romans 14:19
Be of the same mind with one another	Romans 15:5
Accept one another	Romans 15:7
Admonish one another	Romans 15:14
Wait for one another	1 Corinthians 11:33
Care for one another	1 Corinthians 12:25
Serve one another	Galatians 5:13
Bear one another's burdens	Galatians 6:2
Show forbearance to one another	Ephesians 4:1-2
Be kind to one another	Ephesians 4:32
Speak to one another in psalms and hymns and spiritual songs	Ephesians 5:19-20

(continued on next page)

Statement	Reference
Be subject to one another	Ephesians 5:21
Lie not to one another	Colossians 3:9
Bear with one another	Colossians 3:13
Forgive each other	Colossians 3:13
Teach and admonish one another	Colossians 3:16
Increase and abound in love for one another	1 Thessalonians 3:12
Comfort one another	1 Thessalonians 4:18
Encourage one another	1 Thessalonians 5:11
Build one another up	1 Thessalonians 5:11
Encourage one another	Hebrews 3:13
Stimulate one another in love and good works	Hebrews 10:24
Do not speak against one another	James 4:11
Do not complain against one another	James 5:9
Confess your sins to one another	James 5:16
Pray for one another	James 5:16
Love one another	1 Peter 1:22
Be hospitable to one another	1 Peter 4:9
Employ (your gifts) for one another	1 Peter 4:10
Clothe yourselves with humility toward one another	1 Peter 5:5
Greet one another with a kiss of love	1 Peter 5:14
Have fellowship with one another	1 John 1:7
Love one another	1 John 3:11
	1 John 3:23
	1 John 4:7
	1 John 4:11
	1 John 4:12
	2 John 5

A church that desires to reach unsaved and unchurched persons, to incorporate them into its community life, and to direct them to full maturity and productivity in the Christian life will want to take all of these "one another" admonitions to heart. As we work to build these traits into our community life, it is helpful to condense these thirty-eight separate admonitions to five essential characteristic traits of persons in a vital, healthy church with evangelistic impact.

Desire to grow

The first trait of a thriving Christian community is the desire to grow. It is vital that a community of believers sincerely desires to bring unsaved and unchurched persons to Christ and his Church. Just as a married couple in one sense is not a "family" without children, a church is not fully realizing the purposes of God without the desire to have children. Basic to everything else, a church must want to grow.

This seems obvious. Most churches express a desire to grow. But many times the desire we articulate is undermined by the attitudes by which we operate. We talk growth. But we act in ways that frustrate and retard our capacity for growth.

For persons who have never or rarely attended church, coming to church is an uncomfortable and threatening prospect. To help these people overcome these initial fears, an evangelistic church will deliberately and purposefully evaluate its life and patterns with the eyes of an unchurched first-timer. With the help of the newest participants, a church will be able to feel the initial impressions of unchurched persons—and list things which create discomfort and uncertainty for them. Once these things have been identified, a church that is committed to growth will make changes to suit the preferences of newcomers.

In anticipation of the arrival of each of our four daughters, Connie and I made changes in our home. Each stage of our family life has felt right and, before the next child arrived, we couldn't imagine a better family. Until we had experienced it with Brooke, our second daughter, we could not visualize our love extending to include another. Yet in anticipation of each child, we gathered the clothing, rearranged furniture, reworked our priorities and schedules and altered our life. When she arrived, we enlarged our love and care to include another daughter. Within days, we would be working through sibling rivalries and, later, the inevitable scraps and altercations. But the pleasure of our growing family more than compensates for the stresses and strains of four active, growing daughters.

To provide for the comfort and convenience of new persons, most churches will need to initiate changes in almost every area of its life—in worship, in education, in leadership, in priorities, in fellowship activities, in groupings of people. To grow, we need to change some of the things we cherish most about our church!

The normal pattern, of course, is to accommodate the preferences of the people who are already participating in the life of the church. While a church will want to be considerate of everyone, the church that is committed to growth will make a conscious decision to do whatever is necessary to make newcomers comfortable, even when the changes are unsettling.

As a new church without a facility of our own, we have often met in homes where we have enjoyed close, meaningful interaction. One of our new ladies, who appreciated the warm fellowship, commented, "This is *so* good. I'm not sure I want our church to grow. We would lose the intimacy and closeness!" As hard as it was to challenge such heartfelt appreciation, we did just that. We continue to do just that as we rearrange and modify our various group gatherings to accommodate growth.

In your church some "indispensable" Sunday school class leaders and teachers may be reassigned to evangelism, and their classes and groups will feel their loss keenly. Some longstanding church activities may be curtailed or even discontinued, and you may hanker for the "good old days." The teenage children of new converts may be disruptive and bring a "bad influence" into the youth group. New innovations, such as a weekly meeting—designed for gathering and scattering for evangelism—may disrupt our familiar patterns of personal, family and church life.

Growth requires a succession of hard changes and adjustments. When we are confronted with possibilities of uncomfortable and threatening changes, the question we face is not *whether* we want to grow, because most of us would say that we do. The question is: How *much* do we want to grow? When our desire to grow exceeds our desire for anything that may thwart or retard our growth, we are ready—in words *and* in spirit—to grow. And we will!

Ready to work—anywhere

A second trait of a vital Christian community receptive to new converts is a readiness to work. Paul challenged Timothy to do the "work" of an evangelist (2 Tim. 4:5). As the apostle knew so well, the word was well chosen. Evangelism is work. It need not be an overwhelming burden for any one person, but it *is* work. And we must be willing and ready to do our part.

The challenge to work actively in evangelism should not be "dumped" onto persons as an addition to a workload which is already burdensome. Hopefully, a church will recognize the wisdom (and necessity) of releasing workers from current responsibilities so that they can participate in evangelistic initiatives. A church must be willing to delete or curtail existing activities and services to make room for broad participation in evangelistic initiatives. In time your evangelism will provide an expanding pool of workers, and a church can expand its witness and service accordingly.

Even when a church releases persons to work in evangelism as part of a normal amount of witness and service, evangelism is work. Unchurched persons rarely come to us; we must go to them—by telephone, literature distribution, door-to-door canvassing, and friendship initiatives. We must find them. We must become acquainted. We must produce materials. We must send out visitors. We must teach and train evangelistic workers. We must nurture new converts. We must prepare letters, lists, and statistical reports. We must make plans, determine assignments, and direct our evangelistic efforts. We must solve the "problems" created by newcomers who swell our classes and activities, fill our parking lot, and crowd our sanctuary. And all of this is work—plain hard work.

The best attitude with which to approach this multitude of tasks is with a readiness to "pitch in" anywhere! Until our courage and experience grows with experience, we may decline certain tasks. But with this exception, we should be willing to take on any assignment. For many of us this will mean we are "in over our heads" at times. But we need to lay aside our fears and do our best.

Equally important is our readiness to "step aside" and allow a new worker to assume a task we have been doing. Once we have come to enjoy a particular assignment and have gained the assurance that we are doing a good job in it, it can be hard to relinquish it to someone else. Perhaps we may hesitate to step out of a position because our successor may not fulfill the responsibility as well. At other times we may hang on to a job for reasons we would not want to admit—the pleasure of making decisions, the satisfaction of influencing direction, the honor of holding certain positions in the church.

As new converts develop into potential workers, seasoned workers must make room for them on the team and, before long, at the top in decision-making and leadership. The best workers in any church are the ones who are always open to reassignment. An essential attitude of *all* workers in a vital, growing church must be a readiness to *work* and to work *anywhere*. This will mean accepting the challenge of new and unfamiliar assignments. It will mean a wholehearted diligence in doing the work. At some point it will mean moving on, either "up" or "down" to another responsibility. When church workers express this kind of selfless availability, a church will assimilate new members!

Inclusive friendliness

A third trait of an enthusiastic, growing church is inclusive friendliness. The ability of its people to receive persons into its midst with genuine warmth and affection and to make them feel welcome is usually the first measure of a church.

This has always been true. But it may well play a larger role today in our fractured and fragmented society. People are reaching out to authentic community life. They need to feel loved. For any number of reasons, people are drawn into the church more often by the warmth of the relationships than by the brilliance of the preaching.[35] Without minimizing the need for solid intellectual content, we must recognize that people are moved as their relational needs are met.

One of the questions we ask unchurched persons in our door-to-door survey is, "If you were to attend church, what kind of a church would you look for?" By far the most frequent response is "a church where the people are friendly."

Many churches work at friendliness in various ways—with greeters, name tags, recognition of guests, visitor cards, and a guest book. Any of these can be helpful. But above and beyond them all is the resolve of all of the members to be friendly.

A warm greeting, a handshake or hug, the light banter of good friends, the sincere inquiry about recent difficulties—in all of these ways we express warm, caring affection to one another.

One of the men in our congregation was painfully shy as a child. As he grew into manhood he recognized his reserve as a liability and determined to greet people and become acquainted. At first he was uncomfortable initiating conversations, but he forced himself to persist in spite of his discomfort. He concentrated on remembering names, using various associations to recall them. In time his discomfort subsided and his greetings came easily and effortlessly. He genuinely enjoyed meeting people and becoming acquainted with them. By the time I met him (he was in his 60s then) he had mastered the art of inclusive friendliness. He would move among the people at church with warm, open-hearted conversations. He resisted formalized approaches like name tags and official greeters. Far preferable, he said, was for *all* of us to practice inclusive friendliness.

When he visited other churches, he would take pleasure (sometimes, it seemed, undue pleasure) in testing a church's friendliness. Instead of taking the initiative in greeting people, he would wait for them to come to him. Time after time, he would return and describe to me the unfriendliness and aloofness of these churches. He would observe that these churches were friendly enough to one another, but they had ignored him. He would lament, "No wonder they don't grow!" Then he would plunge in again to practice and to inspire us to new levels of warmth and inclusiveness.

At this point a smaller church has the advantage over a large church, because persons can recognize guests easily and greet them appropriately. In the large church this is not possible. We may be greeting one of the "founding fathers" as a newcomer! We must be willing for mistakes that result in making a new acquaintance in the church, whether an "oldtimer" or a first-time guest.

Our friendliness—or lack of it—will frequently be the first impression newcomers will have of our church. More often than not, it will be a greater consideration in people's eventual decision to participate than the quality of the music, the caliber of the message, or the physical surroundings. Like all of us, new converts want to be with people who make them feel welcome and cared for.

Announce good news

A fourth trait of a growing church is a capacity to communicate good news. For many unchurched persons, a church service or activity is an unfamiliar and threatening prospect, and it takes a powerful motivation to induce them to come. In most instances, that motivation is a desire to hear and experience "something more." They may be staggering under the pressures of life or tormented by a nagging dissatisfaction. But their underlying motive is the desire for a better life and, in search of this, they are ready to consider Christ and his Church. When they come, they must hear and feel good news!

Now it is a given that the gospel is good news. The Greek word "evangel" means "good news." Unsaved persons are sure to hear good news in our church, we think, because we "preach the gospel." But will they?

Like cereal, the "gospel" comes in many brands. We use the same Scriptures but, by selective use of favorite themes, we manage to present a "different gospel" from one church to another.

In one church the "gospel" will be announced with an undercurrent of self-discipline. The Bible announces the "good news" for all . . . if we only apply ourselves. Without realizing it, we communicate a "willpower" approach to the Christian life. We emphasize the disciplines of the Christian life at the expense of the transforming power of the grace of God. Believers are encouraged to "feed themselves" through reading, hearing, studying, memorizing and meditating on the Word of God. As we apply ourselves to the disciplines of Bible reading, prayer, worship, witness and service, our lives can be turned around! That *is* good news. But many of the seekers in our services and activities have come precisely because they have been exerting their wills to change—and are failing! They have come to hear the good news of a better way!

In another church the "gospel" will be tainted by legalism. The Bible shows us how we "ought" to live. Biblical teachings for daily life have hardened into rigid standards of right and wrong. The pervasive church mentality is to measure one another by these criteria—and then associate (and disassociate) accordingly. Persons who by their own judgment meet prevailing standards (whether explicit or implicit) communicate a subtle arrogance and condescension. Even without words, new people can sense these attitudes—and are repelled. Often, they have come because they have failed to meet even the modest standards they set for themselves, let alone the unique and lofty ones set by a legalistic church. There is nothing wrong with high biblical standards so long as they are tempered by grace, mercy, kindness, patience, and humility.

In another church the "good news" announced from the pulpit will be undermined by the inconsistency of people's lives. Even while the preacher is expounding on the Scriptures, guests are observing the living "letter[s] . . . known and read by everybody" (2 Cor. 3:2-3). If the kingdom of God, as the pastor is preaching, is "righteousness, peace and joy" in the Holy Spirit, it should be evident in these lives. Where is it? What is it like? Are these people any different from me? Do these people have something more than I do now? These are the questions our guests are asking, and answering, based on the consistency they observe between our message, spoken and lived.

A church that communicates good news announces a message of grace—in the initial acceptance of salvation and throughout the Christian life. Yes, we practice the disciplines of the Christian life, but the desire and ability to practice them is given by the Holy Spirit; always we advance in the transforming power of the grace of God. The biblical standards we teach are not obligations, but opportunities to integrate the good news in a practical way into our lives, and to experience for ourselves the resultant pleasures of righteousness, peace, and joy. Yes, we advocate the highest biblical standards without equivocation, but with a constant awareness of our own vulnerability to failure and the incompleteness of our own ongoing transformation. With that stance, we can be transparent with one another; we can admit our failings, challenge one another in love, and be forgiving and patient. We can affirm our leadership, even while we prayerfully and supportively encourage them to greater character and effectiveness. We have determined that the message we proclaim, and the lives we live, will communicate good news!

Loving care

A fifth trait of a vital, growing church is loving care for one another. This church takes seriously the biblical admonitions to love one another, forgive one another, encourage one another, comfort one another, and to bear one another's burdens. First impressions which bring a newcomer back a second and third time soon give way to lasting observations, based on our capacity to love and serve one another. When their needs are being met, people stay. And in their appreciation and enthusiasm, they invite their family, friends, and neighbors.

Again, church leaders can structure ways to express love—and all of these are helpful. But ultimately, the determining factor in the success or failure of even the best of these initiatives is the capacity of each individual member to love and serve others in the church. Individually, we must make the commitment to love.

Often, the smallest expressions of love are the most appreciated. Just this week one of the men of our church offered to mow our lawn. I had let it go too long, and it had gotten shaggy. My normal workload was doubled by unexpected trauma for one of our families. Guests were coming to our home for the weekend. I was pushing to complete my added responsibilities. And the lawn went unmowed . . . until he volunteered to serve me in this unassuming way.

Another of our men, knowing that one of our families wanted a basketball goal, watched for possibilities. When a friend at work moved into a new home with a goal he wanted to remove, the man got his consent to take the goal. Then he spent a half day, using his own truck and equipment, to dig the well-secured pole out of the ground and transport it to the other family's home. Once the pole was sanded and painted, he spent another half day helping to put it in place.

When one of our families was out of work and out of money, another of our men talked with the family to ascertain the situation and, as accurately as possible, the underlying reasons for the never-ending succession of financial crises—then began to respond. In consultation with me as pastor, he provided financial assistance for the emergency needs—food and utilities. He located new sources of emergency food. Then, sensing that a job driving a taxi might fit the man's experience and propensities, encouraged and helped him to get a chauffeur's license. As a result of the man's labors, the father is driving a taxi now and earning enough money to care for himself and his family.

When this kind of love and caring is extended beyond the inner circle to everyone in the church—even the newest participants—it creates an environment where believers, old and new, flourish and grow into a fully Christian life. The atmosphere is charged with good news. Everyone feels the warm embrace of inclusive friendliness. Participants are eager to pitch in and help at anything. The joy overflows to the surrounding community in active outreach to unchurched friends and neighbors.

People are drawn to a church like this. They stay because their needs are being met. And the word will spread, just as Jesus promised, "All men will know that you are my disciples if you love one another" (John 13:35).

Activities

1. When seekers or converts come among us for the first time, they hear what we say—and they feel who we are. In the early weeks of participation, new persons sense the realities of righteousness, peace, and joy, and are bonded to us. Or they feel the lack of them, and draw back. Describe your initial feelings and impressions when you first began attending your church. If you have grown up in the church, describe your initial reactions in another group that was new to you.

2. Try to "feel" an unchurched person's initial impressions of your congregation. Interview one of the newest participants in your church. Ask the person to recall initial feelings and impressions. List things which were attractive and appealing. Also

record things which created discomfort and uncertainty. What might be done to enhance the initial experiences of guests in your church?

3. Evaluate your own "friendliness quotient." On a scale of 1 to 5 (with 5 representing the best responses), evaluate your readiness to:
— initiate conversations with persons you do not know
— remember names
— talk with as many persons as possible
— respond helpfully to expressed needs
— welcome guests and introduce them to others.

4. Evaluate your church (or group) with "good news" criteria. Is the gospel proclaimed with an undercurrent of willpower? legalism? Is it undermined by inconsistent living? What changes might enhance the "good news" as proclaimed and demonstrated by your group?

5. What attitudes and actions are needed in your congregation to create and/or maintain a healthy, constructive, supportive environment for new converts? What can you do personally to help this happen?

12

Among *All* Peoples

One Saturday I was using an opinion poll to discover unchurched persons in a nearby neighborhood. At one home a dark-skinned couple met me at the door and graciously received me into their home. When I described my survey, his wife responded politely, "We're Hindu. We wouldn't be interested." She paused, then added, "But my mother-in-law is coming to visit us next week. She's a Christian. She will be."

Two weeks later, two East Indian ladies, wearing their *saris*, came to our worship service. To our ears, their English seemed accented. But the limitations of language were readily diffused by smiles.

As our acquaintance grew, we discovered that the mother-in-law, Dora Jesudassen, was a devout believer and active worker in the Church of South India. She spent hours praying. She was diligent in Bible study and memorization, and had learned much of the New Testament by heart. She led Bible studies for up to 300 women. Frequently, couples experiencing difficulties in their marriage relationship would come to Dora for counseling and prayer. At times, praying for people, she would see demons leaving. "They looked like animals," she said, "like pigs and cows, but without feet. . . ."

In the surrounding villages she preached as an evangelist. She distributed food and clothing to the poor. During Holy Week, when seven laypersons were chosen to preach, in turn, on one of Jesus' sayings on the cross, Dora was honored with one of these preaching assignments. Her Christian life, as we learned of it through her halting English and the more fluent elaborations of her daughter-in-law, was a powerful inspiration. Her name,

Jesudassen, which means "disciple of Jesus," was a fitting one.

Just before Mrs. Jesudassen was to return to India, she had a heart attack. During the nine days that she was hospitalized, I visited her in the intensive coronary care unit. As I came into her room she would greet me with a fresh account of the Lord's nearness and goodness and then request particular Scripture passages for me to read. Then we would talk and pray together. Invariably, her buoyant spirits lifted mine.

On the ninth day after her heart attack, Dora died. Anticipating her death, she had insisted that her son not have any Hindu ceremonies. She wanted a Christian burial—and Reverend Hoffman was to officiate.

At Dora's Christian memorial service and burial, I spoke to thirty-five East Indian families, most of them Hindu, a few Muslim, and one or two Christian. All were East Indian immigrants living nearby in the Oklahoma City area.

Following the service, we were invited to the son's home, along with five or six Indian families. Since then, we have been invited to their home several more times. Each time they have had friends there.

Without expecting or seeking it, the Lord has opened a door to the East Indian community here in Oklahoma City. As Dora worshipped with us, we became acquainted with her daughter-in-law, Tilicum, and then her son, Isaac, and her granddaughters, Sheela and Nalini. We discovered a whole new community of people, east Indian immigrants, all around us.

Now we know numbers of East Indians on a first name basis. Isaac and Tilicum attend our church occasionally. Another family attends regularly. These two families are a potential beachhead into an East Indian immigrant population of over 1,000 persons in the Greater Oklahoma City area, most of whom are unsaved and unchurched.

Right here in Oklahoma City, we have the opportunity to be witnesses to persons "from the ends of the earth." And we are not unique. In our increasingly pluralistic society, most churches will have the same opportunity and challenge. The nations of the world are at our doorstep.

Matthew 28:19-20

Jesus' commission to make disciples in Matthew 28:19-20 includes *all* peoples. He commands, "Therefore go and make disciples of all nations. . . ."

Unfortunately, the full extent of Jesus' challenge is obscured by our contemporary use of the word "nations." When we see the word, we think of the two hundred or so nation-states in the world. We visualize political entities with clearly delineated geographical boundaries. The original Greek word, however, does not refer to political/geographical countries, but to the cultural and ethnic groups within them. It describes groups of people with common languages, traits, and customs. In light of contemporary usage, the original Greek word "ta ethne" would be better translated as "peoples" or "people groups."[36]

In our modern world, nations are generally composed of many ethnic or tribal groups. The African nation of Zambia, for example, contains seventy-two different tribes. The nation of India contains 3,500 people groups.

No one knows for sure how many people groups there are in the world. David Barrett, the author of *World Christian Encyclopedia*, is currently developing an atlas which will include 11,000 peoples and languages. The U.S. Center for World Mission lists approximately 22,000 different people groups in the world and reports that, among them, almost 17,000 are still unreached. According to the Greek text, we are commissioned to make disciples among all of these![37]

Most often we think of going "to the ends of the earth" to fulfill this commission. In many cosmopolitan areas, however, we can go to many of the people groups of the world without leaving our own country, city and, at times, even our own street.

This is not a new phenomenon. When Peter preached to the crowd of Jews and Jewish proselytes on the day of Pentecost, he was speaking, in Luke's enumeration, to "Parthians, Medes and Elamites; residents of Mesopotamia, Judea and Cappadocia, Pontus and Asia, Phrygia and Pamphylia, Egypt and the parts of Lybia near Cyrene; visitors from Rome (both Jews and converts to Judaism); Cretans and Arabs" (Acts 2:9-11).

In our day the most obvious place to look for different "peoples" is among immigrants. Apart from our Native Americans, we are a nation of immigrants. The original influx of European immigrants has been largely assimilated into the melting pot of North American culture. But more recent immigrants from Asia and Central and South America are still visible in our cities and communities as distinct language and people groups.

In areas of North America like the Rio Grande Valley and Southern California, or the great "port" cities of Miami, New York, Philadelphia, Baltimore, New Orleans, Houston, Los Angeles, San Francisco, Seattle, Toronto, and Vancouver, the numbers of immigrants are staggering.

The overflow is spilling into communities all across North America. It is common for most of us to meet numbers of international families at school functions, in local sports events, and at neighborhood stores and business. We are surrounded by the peoples of the world in our own communities!

Another place to find the peoples of the world is among international visitors. Over five million non-tourist international visitors come to the United States from 180 countries in the course of a single year. The majority of these visitors are Muslim, Hindu, Buddhist, and Communist.

Perhaps the most accessible group of international visitors is foreign students. At the present time more than 500,000 international students are studying at North American colleges and universities.[38] These students are ripe for friendship. They are eager for exposure to North American people and culture. Often they can benefit from practical assistance of a variety of kinds. Among these students you can do "foreign missions" at home!

In addition, our own culture, like any other, is stratified into innumerable groups of different kinds of people. While they are not necessarily ethnic groupings (though they may be), these groups represent different "peoples" within our own culture. In each group the lifestyle, dialect, music, values, and behavioral patterns are sufficiently different that they are recognized in sociological studies as distinct subcultural groups.

Familiar subcultural groups are children, youth, students, singles, and seniors. Without difficulty we can press beyond these to artists, professional musicians, pilots, delinquents, prisoners, ex-convicts, refugees, and cult members.

An extreme example of one of the subcultures in our towns

and cities is the one we call "street people." This group is composed of teenage runaways, alcoholics, criminals, prostitutes, and those who are intentionally unemployed. Ordinarily, street people have not been successful in any of the typical middle-class ways. They endured school as disgruntled non-achievers, eventually dropped out, and now are unable to hold a steady job. The one thing they do well is "getting by." This may mean heterosexual or homosexual prostitution, selling drugs, stealing, working at brief jobs, and getting handouts. They are not gathering assets for the future. Yesterday is already forgotten and tomorrow will come without thought; they are living for "now." Whatever they are, the means justify the end—which is survival.[39]

Unfortunately, the contemporary evangelical church has focused primarily on a single subcultural group, the middle-class family. Whatever the denomination, the vast majority of our churches provide a wide range of services—preaching, Sunday school, choir, and specialized programs for men, women, children and youth—for a narrow range of people, the middle class family unit.

Frank Tillapaugh writes, "Some time ago the *Home Mission* magazine of the Southern Baptist Convention lamented that over ninety percent of their churches were ministering nearly exclusively to a middle class which makes up about one-third of our cities."[40] Few evangelical denominations can cite any better statistics.

The result is intense competition for middle-class families to the neglect of other people groups in the unchurched population. Many of us, after all, are living in middle-class families—and our first call is to reach out to those persons closest to us. Certainly, we want to work actively to bring our children and youth to personal faith in Christ and full Christian maturity.

But Jesus' great commission does not allow us to stop there. His command is to go to *all* peoples. To fulfill that charge, some will travel to other nations as missionaries. But many more will remain at home in active witness and service to unchurched peoples near us.

We can break the habit of homogeneity. By deliberate and purposeful initiatives, we can break through cultural and sociological barriers to the people groups all around us. If we are to be obedient to the Great Commission as it stands in Scripture and not to a truncated version of our own making, we can do no less!

Evangelism to unreached people groups is not nearly as difficult as we might think. At the simplest, it is a matter of extending our love to particular persons (and families) around us. Then with vision and sociological insight, we can fashion approaches to reach the larger group. Even when our cross-cultural experiences have been negligible, we can witness to—and win!—entire people groups for Christ.

The first step: expanding our vision

The first step is to expand our vision for evangelism to include the unreached people groups around us. Once we realize that we can make disciples of all people, even in our own communities, our vision can be expanded to include whomever we might find close at hand.

Many times, these groups are "invisible." They have been living among us all the time. But when our evangelistic energies are focused only on persons like ourselves, we tend to miss these "other" people. We see them, but we do not recognize them as *our* mission field. We must allow the Holy Spirit to open our eyes and hearts.

Even before we know any individuals by name and need, our vision can be expanded to encompass aggregates of people. With relative ease we can secure population statistics for the various ethnic groups in our city or county. Once our interest here was stirred, we checked with the United States Census Bureau and discovered that in the Greater Oklahoma City area there are approximately 28,000 Hispanics, 26,000 American Indians, and 15,000 Asians.

Beyond this, we can be alert for news about the people groups in our area. While he was attending seminary, Tim Tennent, now a Methodist pastor, was reading a publication called *Unreached Peoples '82* and noticed an unreached people group in his hometown of Atlanta, Georgia. The group, called "Casual Laborers in Atlanta," was described as transient workers picked up off the street to work at night, loading and unloading trucks. Inspired, Tim secured a summer job loading trucks in Atlanta. Then he spent three months in active witness among a group of workers wholly inaccessible to normal daytime ministry, eventually leading one to faith in Christ.[41]

Once we "see" these invisible peoples, we can determine, as individuals and as a church, to reach out to them in our witness. We can purpose, from this time on, not to neglect any of the peoples which the Holy Spirit "assigns" to us.

The second step: caring concern

The next step is to adopt a stance of caring concern. When we expand our vision to include the unreached peoples in our community, we do not plunge in with our own premature initiatives. We wait with caring concern for the direction of the Holy Spirit.

That is, we proceed with our current evangelistic initiatives to people like ourselves, but with a new concern to make contact with unreached peoples. We may wait for weeks or months before we encounter someone in one of these groups. But in the Spirit's time we will meet someone different from ourselves. This person—and the people group they represent—may be the Spirit's particular assignment for us. Once we have established this initial contact, our concern can blossom into active care and service.

Each of our international contacts has occurred "accidentally" as we were contacting families in the area. In one, I was calling through a list of new families and one woman responded in halting English. Her husband, I understood her to say, was a student at Oklahoma University. The couple, with their two children, were living in a nearby apartment. Even in the halting words and phrases, her eagerness for friendship and Bible study was unmistakable. When I suggested our worship service as a good initial exposure, I was introduced to the process of cross-cultural discovery which was to characterize the next six months. She replied, "I will talk with my husband. If he approves, we will come."

Either Eriko was persuasive or Kaoru was receptive, because the next Sunday morning when I drove to the apartment to lead them along unfamiliar streets to our meeting place, the family was radiant with anticipation.

Even though their religious background was Buddhist, they

were eager to meet new American friends and ready for their first exposure to the Christian faith.

For the next six months this delightful Japanese family participated in the life of our congregation. We learned that Kaoru was a highly specialized "student," a pediatric cardiologist, doing research at the Oklahoma University Medical Center. Eriko, we discovered, had been graduated from a university in Japan with a major in American literature. Coming to the United States was a dream come true for her. For both of them, it was a chance to learn the Christian faith firsthand.

Before the Yoshiis left Oklahoma City for more study in Boston, our warm association culminated with their profession of faith, public testimony, and Christian baptism! It was a glorious introduction to the appeal of cross-cultural evangelism.

Another contact began just as providentially. A missionary friend in New Mexico had written to tell us that a former student, a Navajo Indian, was living in the Oklahoma City area with her family. I found the family and discovered that Priscilla's faith, while suffering from neglect, was intact. Her husband Peter's was negligible at best. In the ensuing weeks we cultivated our friendship with the family. When we began a Bible study nearby, we invited them to attend. To our surprise, Peter became an eager participant in the study. As a result of the weekly stimulation of the book of Mark, he came to an active, personal faith in Christ. After moving several times within the city, they are now attending our church regularly.

There are so many unreached peoples all around us that we cannot help but discover them. When we do, an initial contact can blossom into full friendship. Invariably, as we care for individual persons and families, we will discover the larger people group of which they are a part.

The third step: fashioning a strategy

As our relationship deepens and our understanding grows, we can look for ways to meet and serve the friends, family, and acquaintances of our initial international friends. In time, we can fashion an evangelistic strategy to reach the people group they represent.

Usually, it is not hard to serve international friends. One

man in our congregation, a university professor, taught international students how to drive. In his association with international students, he discovered that they, and particularly their wives, often have difficulty learning to drive in the United States. The husbands would often learn how and then try to convey their new skill to their wives. After a few frustrating attempts they would give up in exasperation. With their patriarchal logic they reasoned, "Why does my wife need to drive anyway?"

This man responded to this need, sometimes at considerable personal risk! He provided a greatly appreciated service, and established a potential evangelistic contact among numbers of international students at Oklahoma University.

As we develop approaches and strategies, we must do so with a readiness to accommodate unfamiliar needs—and to make adjustments in church-life-as-usual. Up to the time that the Yoshiis began worshipping with us, I had preached from a full outline. My notes were extensive, but my delivery extemporaneous. After a week of study and preparation, my amplifications on the outline were hidden away in my mind. In a short time we learned that both Dr. and Mrs. Yoshii were adept at reading written English. But spoken English was new to them, especially for Eriko. So from then on, I prepared a complete manuscript of my message and delivered it to the Yoshiis on Friday or Saturday. Even though my delivery on Sunday morning was still largely extemporaneous, the Yoshiis had the advantage of listening to a message they had already read. It gave them a chance to practice their English listening skills. And it enhanced their understanding of the biblical concepts I wanted to communicate. Since the Yoshiis have returned to Japan, I have learned that Eriko kept each of these messages and they are now circulating (for better or worse) in Bible studies in Japan!

These intuitive responses are often "right on target" as we respond to a new people group. In addition, we can draw upon the insights of specialists in parachurch organizations. Most of these organizations concentrate on a particular group of people in an intense, comprehensive way. Campus Crusade for Christ and InterVarsity concentrate on students. The Navigators developed initially from a ministry to sailors and servicemen. Teen

Challenge concentrates on delinquents. Prison Fellowship focuses on prisoners. Covenant House specializes in runaways.

Each of these ministries has developed specialized skills in working with a particular people group. They have discovered attitudes and approaches which are effective for witness and evangelism among their particular target audience.

We can benefit from their accumulated wisdom by asking pertinent questions: What kind of staff does a group utilize? What kind of training are workers given? What needs do they work to meet? What approaches have been proven effective for them? What attitudes do they encourage among their workers? How do they contact these persons initially? What meeting places are working best for them?

As we consider a particular organization's strategies, not all of them may be feasible in our circumstances. But even in these instances, we are broadening our exposure to various approaches and, in the process, discovering what will fit our sensitivities and proclivities.

As we actively work to familiarize ourselves with a particular target group, and then learn from our own experiences and from parachurch specialists, we can shape the evangelistic strategy we will use. Few strategies will emerge full-blown in our initial planning. But even the rudiments of a strategy will enable us to begin. Once started, the adjustments and refinements of our approaches will follow, no doubt with the frustrations of trial and error. But they *will* come.

The fourth step: fielding a team

Once we catch a vision for witness to unreached peoples, we will want to advance beyond our initial emotional fervor to identify particular target groups, to fashion a strategy and, finally, to field a team. Then we are in earnest about attaining our full evangelistic potential as a church!

The final step is a "check point" for organizing an initiative to a new people group. Are any church members actively interested? Are persons ready to invest themselves in a witness to a particular group?

A church with a vision for unreached peoples will release

members from current assignments so that they can concentrate their energies on reaching these people. This may involve a modification of the church budget to provide financial support. As a ministry develops, it may lead to the employment of a specialized staff person. For years now our congregations typically have sought specialists for various programs which serve the middle-class family—pastor, associate pastor, Christian education director, music director, and youth pastor. Can we conceive of an initiative to an unreached people group developing to the point that we assign a street pastor? a refugee pastor? a pastor working exclusively with international students?

Evangelism to the invisible peoples in our communities is a bold and challenging venture. It is also one of the most deeply satisfying. As we continue to correspond with Kaoru and Eriko Yoshii in Japan, we marvel at the tenacity of their developing faith. Eriko has been hosting Bible studies in her home, first with a missionary teacher, and now with a Japanese pastor. Now this initial study has developed into two studies. With the family's relocation to another part of Fukoaka City "where there is no church," Eriko reports, another section of Japan has a potentially active Christian witness.

As I look out over our own congregation on a Sunday morning, I see persons from Navajo, Vietnamese, East Indian, Japanese, and African extraction. We include persons from Hindu, Buddhist, and Animistic backgrounds. We encompass minority groups, pilots, singles, young adults, handicapped persons, professionals, and blue collar workers—and their families.

Even as I write now, Connie is preparing a meal for a young family we met three weeks ago. Richard and Adele are from Zimbabwe. We discovered them by word of mouth through a friend in Kansas. At our invitation they came to church. Now we are beginning the process of becoming acquainted, discerning interests and needs, and responding with friendship and service. As a family—and a church—we are in the midst of an exciting cross-cultural adventure.

When I reflect on this, and realize that all this has happened without our ever leaving Oklahoma City, it is highly motivating to press on with more and greater initiatives to "make disciples among *all peoples*."

Activities

1. In our increasingly pluralistic society, most churches have the opportunity to be witnesses to persons "from the ends of the earth." Identify the different "peoples" in your own community. Are there immigrants? international students? Are there subcultural groups that churches do not appear to be reaching?

2. Gather demographic data on the various ethnic groups in your area. Contact the United States Census Bureau or Statistics Canada for information. In the United States, write to the Glenmary Research Center (750 Piedmont Ave., N.E., Atlanta, GA 30300) and request a "Ten Fact Sheet" for the counties served by your church. How many persons live in your area? Where do they live? Are they served by any churches?

3. List the persons in your congregation (or study group), including occasional participants, and identify the ethnic/cultural background of each. Is there a cluster of persons having a similar background? Are there persons whose background is significantly different from a majority of others in the group? As well as you can, identify the expressed needs, aspirations, and sensitivities of those who might feel somehow "out-numbered." What steps can be taken to build full friendships? to respect cultural differences? to serve the needs of everyone in the group?

4. If there are persons in your congregation whose ethnic/cultural background is significantly different from that of the majority of your congregation, they most likely are part of larger people groups in your community. Write down as much as you know about the size, location, religious affiliations, cultural patterns, needs, and aspirations of these groups in the community. Are you drawn to a particular group? Does your church have resources which would enable you to offer witness and service to a particular group? What initiatives might be possible at this point?

13

A Truly Great Church

Less than a year ago, one of our evangelistic teams met with Jay and Jessie in their home for the first time. Jay sat quietly, with a demeanor that communicated grudging participation. Jessie talked easily, but her hesitant glances at Jay suggested that they had not openly discussed their faith in all the years of their marriage.

In our conversation we learned that both had a nominal church experience as children and then had drifted away. In their 40s now, they had not been attending church for years. In response, one of our team shared personal stories of God's action in his life. We described our church, invited them to worship with us, and prayed briefly.

Two weeks later Jessie came to our worship service. The next week Jay came with her. They chose to participate in our class for new Christians, though I was not at all sure they qualified at the time. By the time we finished the class, however, both were committed to a restoration of their relationship with the Lord.

During the next six months, Jay and Jessie listened attentively to the sermons and participated actively in small group discussions. Some of the biblical concepts were new to Jay and Jessie and challenged them to a deeper level of Christian commitment than they had known. Yet they considered each one and quietly began to reshape their living by new convictions.

I was accustomed to their rapt attention when I preached my annual recruitment message for RESCUE (see p. 136), our evangelistic initiative. But I did not anticipate their response at the end when I invited anyone who wanted to work in evangelism to stand. To my surprise, Jay stood. Within moments, Jessie joined him.

From the start, Jay and Jessie participated eagerly in our RESCUE work. As I taught the fundamentals of evangelism week by week they listened carefully and practiced each successive skill eagerly. Though they were not comfortable praying aloud at the time, they wanted to learn how to pray for evangelism. From their own experience, they confirmed the necessity of encouragement. They listened carefully as I explained the benefit of sharing personal stories, then shared stories of their own which could be shaped into a personal testimony. They participated enthusiastically in home visits, and readily spoke about what the Lord was doing in their lives. They were ready to try their hand at telephone calling which, for some, is the most threatening of all the things we do. In everything, they expressed a sense of joy that, after such a long lapse in faith, they could again be serving the Lord.

With the insights that they were gaining in our evangelistic training, they began to talk with family members about their renewed faith. They talked about their faith on the job with co-workers and in their recreational pursuits with friends. As they shared, they invited these persons to church. Their sons came with their families and, in time, one began to attend regularly.

As I observed their excitement and pleasure in evangelism, I marveled at what was happening. Just six months before, they were unchurched themselves. Now they were eagerly bringing others to Christ and the church.

By this time, our congregation was making decisions about leadership for the next year. One responsibility we needed to fill was RESCUE coordinator (leader). We considered the various persons on the team, including Jay and Jessie. Even though they were among our newest participants, they had been enthusiastic and faithful in RESCUE. They had been avid learners, and had actively applied their new insights. They were appreciated and respected by others on the team. Their obvious interest and earnest involvement, along with the evident effectiveness of their witness, seemed to indicate both the inclination and aptitude for evangelistic work. And they had, we felt, good leadership skills. We nominated Jay and Jessie to lead our evangelistic team as

RESCUE coordinators. The congregation approved and, with a prayer of dedication, they were "sent" to serve the Lord in a major leadership responsibility in the work of our church.

Under Jay and Jessie's leadership, our RESCUE team is actively reaching out to unchurched persons. Members are making exciting initiatives to unchurched friends and acquaintances. We are experiencing a steady stream of guests in our services and activities. Persons are praying to receive Christ. New persons are attending our services regularly. With all of this, our church is thriving—growing—as the Lord intends.

In less than a year, Jay and Jessie have come full circle in our evangelistic work. They were reached. They were taught and equipped. Now they have been sent out in witness and service—and the same progression is being duplicated in other lives as a result of their work.

To be sure, Jay and Jessie are still developing in their renewed faith. Even as they work in evangelism, they are building new biblical patterns of living. The process is by no means complete.

But the fact remains: Jay and Jessie exemplify the success we strive for in our evangelistic work. They have been captured by Christ. They are being remade according to his Word. And they have been redirected into his service. When the Lord is doing this in our midst, we consider ourselves to be a truly great church.

Does that remark surprise you? Sound like boasting? Let me tell you why I say that, and why I think that all of us can experience the thrill of being part of a truly great church.

It certainly is not because our congregation is a large church. We do not have a big budget. As this book is being written, we do not even have a permanent facility. Our people (and pastor) are flawed and incomplete. We do not have a radio or television ministry. We are not doing anything unique that another congregation couldn't do as well.

But being a truly great church is not dependent on having a permanent place for worship. It doesn't depend on a particular group of people, or on having an exceptional pastor. From a biblical perspective, being a truly great church depends on the congregation's outlook, a perspective given by the Holy Spirit.

The Bible talks about a number of great churches. But the

church in Antioch stands head and shoulders above them all. In Acts 11 we learn that the church in Antioch was a young church. To use a contemporary term, it was a "church planting." The church included people from a diversity of backgrounds. Likely, they had no permanent facility. Their pastor had never pastored a church before. Yet they were, I suggest, the greatest church in the whole of the New Testament because they had the outlook, the attitudes, the perspectives which characterize a truly great church.

Reaching the unreached

First, they were reaching the unreached. Up to this time, believers had only talked to Jewish people. Likely, it never occurred to anyone to talk to Gentiles because the Jews hated the Gentiles; they didn't think the Gentiles had any interest in God or that God had anything worthwhile for them. They were un-reached, and no one wanted to reach them either.

But at Antioch, for the first time in the history of the church, believers were sharing the gospel with the Gentiles. "Now those who had been scattered by the persecution in connection with Stephen traveled as far as Phoenicia, Cyprus and Antioch, telling the message only to Jews. Some of them, however, men from Cyprus and Cyrene, went to Antioch, and began to speak to Greeks also, telling them the good news about the Lord Jesus. The Lord's hand was with them, and a great number of people believed and turned to the Lord" (Acts 11:19-21).

The church in Antioch had an outlook, a concentration, a perspective, a purpose to reach out to people who had not been reached. And it literally changed the world. A truly great church always has that kind of attitude.

I wish you could have seen Candra when she came to church for the first time. As she walked in the door her face was covered with fear. Her eyes were darting back and forth. There were beads of perspiration on her forehead. She told us later she'd had a couple of drinks before she came, to get up her courage. She sat in the back—as far back as she could. She stayed at the edge of the crowd. Never once did she let me get between her and the door. And as soon as church was over—whoosh, she was gone. That excites me. When people come to church like that, it's obvious that we're reaching the unreached.

The Bible doesn't say that heaven rejoices over one believer that changes churches. It says heaven rejoices over one sinner that repents. That's where the action is. That's where the excitement is.

Last fall I was in San Diego at a conference that was held at a church which began as a church planting some thirty years ago. The founding pastor spoke the first night about the early days of that church. Someone had provided a church facility, he said, the first church building in the new housing development. He had a background in advertising which he used to good effect to promote the new church. By the time the first church service was held, there were 200 people in attendance. But only a handful were believers. Numbers of persons, pressed into service as Sunday school teachers, weren't even Christians yet! And the youth group was the bane of the local police force.

At the time, the pastor explained, that area had the highest crime and delinquency rate in San Diego. Every time they had a church service there would be two or three police cars in the parking lot. The pastor would come out of the service and his youth group would be lined up against the wall. The police would be frisking them. Invariably, the police would take two or three of his youth away.

It got so bad that a few families in the church—the pillars, the few who were believers—came to the pastor. They said, "We can't take this anymore. Our kids are in that youth group. We can't have our children with that kind of kids. You are going to have to make a choice: it's either us or those kids." The pastor went home and agonized in prayer, "Lord, what do I do?"

When the Lord showed him, he went back to the pillars of his church and said, "You folks know the Lord. You've already accepted him into your life. If you leave this church, you'll find your way into another church, and in time you'll find your way into heaven. But those kids don't know the Lord. They're not saved. If they leave here, they won't find their way to another church. If you go, you go with my blessing. But I've got to stick with these kids."

That church today has 3,000 people on Sunday mornings.

It's a great church. But it was great even then—because that pastor had an attitude to reach the unreached.

So the first mark of a truly great church is that it's a church that's reaching the unreached.

Equipping the unequipped

The second mark of a truly great church is that it is equipping the unequipped. When we think of the Apostle Paul, we think of a great apostolic missionary. We think of his gifts, his hard work, and his success. But in Acts 11, he was not yet Paul; he was still called Saul. By reputation he was a persecutor. He had hounded Christians from house to house and town to town to throw them into prison, some to be killed. He was brilliant, but abrasive.

Yet Barnabas saw in Saul the untapped potential of a mighty evangelist. So we read, "Then Barnabas went to Tarsus to look for Saul, and when he found him, he brought him to Antioch" (Acts 11:25). As Barnabas and Saul worked together, Barnabas poured his life into this young firebrand. He taught him, trained him, encouraged him, affirmed him. No doubt he also rebuked him and corrected him. By the end of only one year of intensive teaching and training, Saul was equipped to be an apostle—because Barnabas and the church in Antioch had the outlook and the perspective to equip the unequipped.

When I was at the San Diego conference, the church people provided hospitality for us in their homes. I happened to be in a home in the Mount Helix area, one of a handful of exclusive areas in San Diego. As I was taking a walk through the area, I noticed the homes and the landscaping. The homes were incredibly beautiful! Many had a view of the ocean, and, if the sky was clear, a view of Mexico. My hostess, a realtor, answered my question about the value of these homes. "We bought our home for $200,000 and now it's worth $400,000. The homes that are higher up on the hill are worth more—$500,000, $700,000 . . . $1,000,000."

One morning as I walked among those beautiful homes, I noticed a couple of empty, unimproved lots with bare dirt, scrubby bushes, and discarded bottles. I was struck by the contrast between those lots and the magnificent homes. I thought,

"What an amazing transformation—from that ugly lot to that magnificent home."

To make a spiritual application, when we come to the Lord, we are all unimproved lots. We may have a great deal of potential, like an ocean view. But we are still an empty lot. A church's opportunity and responsibility is to take an "empty lot" and to build on it a $400,000 person, a $500,000 person, a $1,000,000 person. The church's responsibility is to equip the unequipped.

At the time of this insight I had to confess I hadn't been equipping like I should have been. How did I know? I was at the home of one of our families once and overheard a phrase that they use with their daughter. When Melissa wonders whether or not she should do something, her parents say to her, "Would Warren do that?" I don't feel badly that they single me out. I think a pastor should be a standard to his people. But why did they choose me and nobody else? They ought to be able to say to Melissa, "Would Dave do that? Would Dan do that? Would Larry do that? Would Cara do that? Would Jamie do that? Would *I* do that?" If I had been doing my job, Melissa's parents would be able to single out numbers of persons in our congregation and say, "Melissa, think twice about that. Would (fill in any name) do that?" The Lord convicted me during that walk through the Mount Helix area and I determined to do a better job in equipping the unequipped.

Sending the "unsendable"

When a church is reaching the unreached and equipping the unequipped, it won't be long before it is expressing a third characteristic—sending the "unsendable." In Acts 13:1, we read, "In the church at Antioch there were prophets and teachers: Barnabas, Simeon called Niger, Lucius of Cyrene, Manean (who had been brought up with Herod the Tetrarch) and Saul." As this group of leaders was worshipping and praying, the Lord singled out Saul and Barnabas, saying in effect, "I want these two to do a special work for me."

Do you realize what the Lord did? He took Barnabas—the founding pastor, the senior pastor, the one that the church relied on, looked up to and depended on for leadership. And he took Saul—the pastor in training, the most promising assistant in the whole church. The Lord took the best. He took the ones who were most fully equipped, the ones who were indispensable, the ones who were "unsendable."

How do you think that church felt? They immediately began to fast and pray. That might be an indication of how they felt! But once they were assured that the Holy Spirit was indeed directing, they laid their hands on them, blessed them and sent them off. All this, because they were committed to send the "unsendable."

I remember the day when I left my home in Pennsylvania to go to seminary in California. I had my '67 Chevelle loaded. Everything was ready. My family was gathered around me. We were kissing, hugging, crying, and praying. I remember how we felt. My family paid a price to let me go—my parents' only son, my sisters' favorite brother. But it's because my family paid the price of sending the "unsendable" that our church is here today.

I think of the times I have challenged persons to leave one class or Bible study to form the nucleus for a new one. In the ensuing discussions I could always sense how hard it is to be sent out.

It's hard to leave the closeness, the support, the comfort and the affection that we enjoy when we're together in a Bible study, Sunday school class, or church fellowship. It feels good. We don't want to leave because it's tough out there. It won't feel the same. It's a lonely feeling, a fearful feeling. It's a heart-wrenching feeling.

But if we will pay that price, the Lord will take what we enjoy at one place and duplicate it in new places. That's how the gospel spreads. When we are willing to be sent out from our Sunday school class, the joy of the gospel will start in our new class. When we are willing to leave our Bible study and go to another, it will start in that Bible study. When we are willing to leave our present church and go to help start another church, it will start there. But we pay a price to be sent out.

A truly great church is not known by the number of persons it receives into membership, by the amount of money it receives in offerings, or by the amount of publicity it receives in church or secular media. It is known by what it gives.

The Lord does not intend for churches to be reservoirs. He intends for them to be like rivers—flowing in, flowing out.

By these criteria, a truly great church can be any size and in any place. Your church can be truly great. It will be great when *you* adopt the perspective to reach the unreachable, to equip the unequipped, and to send out the "unsendable."

That will mean a personal commitment to participation in evangelism. I promised you in the introduction that, if you have the will, I would show you a way to work in evangelism. I have done my best to fulfill that promise by describing the diversity of abilities which contribute to the work of evangelism. Whether you have an aptitude for prayer, encouragement, telling personal stories, presenting the gospel, teaching, writing, typing, or leading, there is a way you can contribute. All that remains is a clear commitment to do so.

Initially, you may be alone in your determination to evangelize. But conviction of any kind is contagious. An earnest band of aspiring evangelists, however small, will have an infectious impact on your entire church. But even if the initial team is small, and the initial results are mixed, you have adopted the first and most important attitude of a truly great church. You are committed to reach the unreached.

It will be crucial to channel the initial enthusiasm for evangelism into substantive training. Otherwise, it will dissipate and disappear when your good intentions bump up against the first obstacles and disappointments.

This book has been designed to help you to do just that. It can provide the teaching component in an initial training course for evangelism. Each chapter has presented a basic concept, usually in connection with a basic skill, that can be applied immediately in the work of evangelism.

If you have thought of this book as a tool box, all the essential tools for evangelism are included—as sort of a "starter kit." As you have grasped the concepts and practiced the skills, you are becoming equipped for your first initiatives in evangelism.

It is essential that you present yourself to be sent out to do the work of evangelism, with whatever contribution you can make. Few of us need to expand our knowledge of evangelism. We already know far more than we are able to do. The aim of this book has been to inform and to motivate, so that you can take action, with a team, to evangelize the unchurched persons in your community.

In broad sweeps, the attitudes of reaching the unreached, equipping the unequipped, and sending the "unsendable" are what mark a truly great church. It took a persecution to blast the church of Jerusalem out of its lethargy.

But the church of Antioch *chose* to do these things. That's what we want to do. We can adopt these perspectives right now—and become the salt that permeates an entire church with the savor of evangelism. As others join us, we can be the vanguard of a mighty moving of God—yes, in our church and in our community.

We may not experience dramatic success. Our church may not explode to a membership in the hundreds and thousands. But if we are following the biblical directives of reaching, equipping and sending, the Spirit will honor our readiness to work by biblical directives, and the kingdom of God will be extended through our efforts. We will enjoy the challenge and fulfillment of being where the action is, of being active participants in building a truly great church.

Activities

1. You can experience the thrill of participating in a truly great church. No, not by moving to a more receptive community. Not by hiring an extraordinary pastor. Not by trading away a few church members and replacing them with better ones. But by developing an outlook of reaching, equipping, and sending people your church can be truly great. Are you persuaded that, if you will do this, your church will be "where the action is"?

2. Reflect on your aspirations as a church. How do you currently envision "success"? By what criteria do you measure faithful witness and service? Identify your aspirations as a church. Now translate these goals into realistic objectives in terms of reaching, equipping, and sending people.

3. This study began with a bold promise: if you have the will, there is a way for you to participate in the work of evangelism. In these thirteen chapters (and accompanying activities) you have been introduced, one by one, to the various abilities which contribute to the work of evangelism. At this point, which seems to be your most likely contribution to the work of evangelism? Prayer? Initial contacts with unchurched persons? Telling personal stories to others? Presenting the gospel? Teaching? Encouragement? Leadership? Behind-the-scenes support? Enhancing congregational life? Cross-cultural initiatives?

4. Consider the opportunity of establishing an ongoing evangelistic team for your church or group. Develop a summary sheet (like the one on Worksheet 16, p. 236) to describe your evangelistic team. If you want, develop an acronym to name your team. Lay the groundwork for invitation and commitment to work with the team. Plan a dedication service for persons who commit themselves to work as an evangelistic team. Go back and reread this book for ideas, direction, and specific actions. Plunge in to the adventure of evangelism!

Worksheets

At the end of each chapter, activities are suggested to provide practice in the basic skills of evangelism. On the following pages are worksheets which will help in conducting studies, developing personal stories, and accomplishing evangelistic tasks.

In addition, the worksheets may be helpful as you prepare a notebook for your evangelistic team. They have been laid out in such a way that they can be photocopied for use in a loose-leaf notebook sized for 5 1/2 inch by 8 1/2 inch pages. (You may have the best success in photocopying if you first carefully cut the worksheet pages out of an extra book, then photocopy them.) Any of these worksheets may be reproduced without obtaining reprint permission. They also can be enlarged for use as overhead projector transparences.

In our congregation we have purchased an inexpensive vinyl notebook, with 1 inch rings, for each worker on our evangelism team. The notebook with the photocopied worksheets provides a quick review of our basic approaches and a convenient way to record prayer requests, appointments, notes on visits, and the other pertinent information which we need on a weekly basis. Since we have the additional aim of building *esprit de corps* among our team members, we took the step of having each person's name embossed on the cover in gold letters, along with RESCUE, the acronym of our evangelistic initiative (*R*eaching, *E*quipping, *S*ending: *C*alling the *U*nchurched to *E*ternal Life).

Worksheet 1

For use with Chapter 1

The Potential Harvest

A motivating step toward active, intentional evangelism is to calculate the number of unchurched persons in your area.

First gather current population statistics. In most instances, it is possible to get statistics for cities, counties, school districts, townships and boroughs—whatever the census divisions are in your area. Normally, these are available from governmental offices, newspapers, or the Chamber of Commerce.

A second statistic you will need is the percentage of unchurched persons in your county. In the United States this statistic is available from the Glenmary Research Center, an agency affiliated with the United States Catholic Conference, which compiles demographic data pertinent to religious groups. Write to the center at 750 Piedmont Ave., NE, Atlanta, GA 30308. Or call (404) 876-6518. Request a *Ten Facts* sheet for the counties within range of your church.

In Canada similar statistics are available from Statistics Canada, the statistical agency of the Canadian government. Call (613) 951-8116 and ask for the religious preferences of persons in your area. For metropolitan areas with a population over 50,000, this information is available in a publication titled *Census Metropolitan Areas with Components: Population, Occupied Private Dwellings, Private Households and Census and Economic Families in Private Households* (catalogue number 95-943). Ask for "population by religion." Information for counties, cities, towns, and villages with smaller populations is contained in the publication *Census Divisions and Subdivisions with Components: Population, Occupied Private Dwellings, Private Households and Census and Economic Families in Private Households* (catalogue number 95-983 through 95-994). This same information is contained on microfiche (number SDC81B16). You will need to calculate your own percentages from the population totals.

(It is important to note that Canadian statistics are based on the religious preference reported by the individuals themselves in the national census. The Glenmary statistics, by contrast, are based on membership statistics received directly from churches. The percentage of churched persons in Canadian statistics, therefore, tends to be higher, reflecting the number of inactive adherants who profess church membership.)

Once you have these two statistics, you can calculate the number of unchurched persons in your community. Multiply the population of your area by the percent of unchurched population in the county. There will be varying concentrations of unchurched persons within any given county, but the resultant figure will provide a helpful approximation of the number of unchurched persons in your area.

Example:

Population of Abilene, Kansas—7500
Population of Dickenson County, Kansas—23,400
Percentage of population unchurched—33.9%
Number of unchurched persons in Abilene—2542
Number of unchurched persons in Dickenson County—7933

This statistic reminds us that, even with the number of churches in our communities, the job is not finished. Many people—thousands and thousands of persons—are still living apart from Christ and regular fellowship with his Church. The statistic for the number of unchurched persons in your area should puncture the assumption that "practically everyone" in our community is participating in church. Jesus' statement in the first century is still true today, "The harvest is plentiful . . . " (Matt. 9:37).

Worksheet 2

For use with Chapter 2

Evangelistic Prayer

One effective way to participate in the work of evangelism is through prayer. The Bible assures us that "when we ask, we will receive" (John 16:24; Matt. 7:7-11).

At least twelve different evangelistic prayers (or requests for prayer) are recorded in the New Testament. These twelve prayers express the revealed will of God in our evangelistic endeavors. They become the normative pattern for our prayers. When our prayers take on the breadth and depth of these prayers, they will be more effective. "If we ask anything according to his will, he hears us. And if we know that he hears us—whatever we ask—we know that we have what we asked of him (1 John 5:14-15).

Let's pray the same way the early church prayed and watch what happens!

1.	Pray to enlist workers	Matthew 9:35-38; Luke 10:2
2.	Pray for the Holy Spirit	Acts 1:4-5, 8, 14
3.	Pray for boldness	Acts 4:29; Ephesians 6:19-20
4.	Pray for signs and wonders	Acts 4:30
5.	Pray for opportunities	Colossians 4:3
6.	Pray for words	Ephesians 6:19
7.	Pray for clarity	Colossians 4:4
8.	Pray for active witnessing	Philemon 6
9.	Pray for rapid spread of the gospel	2 Thessalonians 3:1
10.	Pray for deliverance	Romans 15:30-32
		2 Thessalonians 3:2-3
		Philippians 1:19
		Hebrews 13:19
		2 Corinthians 1:8-11
11.	Pray for support of workers	1 Thessalonians 5:25
		Hebrews 13:18
12.	Pray for the salvation of particular persons	Romans 10:1

Worksheet 3

For use with Chapter 3

Finding Newcomers

An initial step in evangelism is to find unchurched persons among the total population. One of the obvious sources of unchurched persons is newcomers in the community. Before you contact them, you must devise a way of finding newcomers as they move into your community.

Establish a word-of-mouth system. Encourage persons in your group to report persons or families who have recently moved into your community.

Find a newcomers greeting service. Look in the Yellow Pages of the telephone book under such headings as "welcome," "greeting," "newcomers" or "list services." Or look in the white pages of the telephone book for familiar services such as Welcome Wagon, Hi Neighbor, or New Neighbor. If you cannot find any, contact the local Chamber of Commerce and ask whether there is a newcomers list service in the community. In an area without a chamber, ask persons who know the community well— the postmaster, bankers, editor of the local newspaper, and local officials.

Cultivate basic sources of information. In a community that does not have a greeting service, you will have to do your own research. Think through the process of moving into your community. What must people do to establish a residence? Typically, newcomers must contact utilities, the post office, schools, the telephone company, banks, newspaper, and medical services. Often they will use moving van companies, make real estate transactions, or contact apartment managers. Not all of these will give out lists of new residents, but some will become good sources of information about newcomers in your community.

Worksheet 4

For use with Chapter 3

Telephone Guide

A telephone call is often a good way to contact newcomers intitially. It is good to begin with a brief explanation for the call. A format which has worked well is:

Hello, *(their name).* This is *(your name).* I'm with one of the churches in this area, the *(give the name of your church).* I've just learned that you're new, or fairly new, in this area (pause) and I'm just calling to see whether you've found a church yet and, if not, to find out whether we can be helpful to you.

After this introduction, the conversation will often take one of several typical directions. Here are some of the most frequent comments with responses we use in Oklahoma City. You will need to adapt several of them to your own church and community.

———————

No, we're still looking . . .
What kinds of things are you looking for?
Friendliness, good Bible teaching, activities for the children.
I think we may be able to serve you. *(Elaborate on the strengths of your church.)* We would be pleased to drop by and tell you more about our church and talk together about ways we may be able to serve you. Would it be convenient this coming Wednesday evening around 8 o'clock?

———————

What did you say your church was again?
(Say the name of your congregation again.)
I've never heard of that church.
(Here we give a brief introduction to our denomination, and then say:)
We invite persons to accept Jesus Christ as Savior and Lord.

We build our faith and practice on the Bible.

We support and care for one another as a close-knit family of believers.

We pray expectantly—and see God act in our lives.

We are eager to serve persons in need.

And the result is a warm, caring, earnest and exciting group of believers!

(Elaborate by sharing a personal "church testimony." Describe the things you appreciate about your church, such as friendliness, music, practical Bible preaching and teaching, children's activities, etc. We often share that we are a young church, just getting started, meeting at the local YWCA. . . .)

Well, I'm (names a denomination) and my husband is (names another denomination), and we haven't been able to agree on a church.

We may be able to help you. We have persons from a number of different church backgrounds in our church, including some from *(list several different church backgrounds represented in your congregation).* As we study the Bible together, everyone brings concerns and emphases from their own background, and we are learning from one another how to apply and live the truth in the Bible. May we drop by and talk more about what you are looking for and share ways we may be able to serve both of you? Would it be convenient this coming Wednesday evening around 8 o'clock?

Yes, we would like to get together, but this week is full.

That's no problem. Would next Wednesday evening be better, around the same time? *(If yes, schedule an appointment. If no, try for Tuesday or Thursday and schedule an appointment.)*

We're (names a denomination) . . .

Are you looking specifically for a (name denomination) church or are you open to another church that would meet your needs?

We've always been (names denomination) and we want a (name denomination) church.

That's great! Have you found the (name denomination) churches near you? *(If they are not familiar with the churches or have not heard of one nearer to them, inform them of churches of that denomination that are nearby.)*

We've already found a church.

Great! Which one have you found?! *(pause for answer; then affirm the church in whatever way you can, and conclude)* I wish you the best! *(If it is a cult or group you cannot affirm, simply wish them the best.)*

No, we're really too busy for a visit. It will work better for us just to come by for a visit . . .

That's great! We meet at the Ione Branch YWCA, on 58th Street between MacArthur and Rockwell at 10 o'clock on Sunday morning. I'll be there to greet you at the door!

(This response is generally a way of putting us off. But respond graciously, as if you believe them. If the persons seems especially sincere, you may want to send a directional brochure.)

We're not interested.

I wish you the best.

Worksheet 5

For use with Chapter 3

Appointments

Month ———————————

Request an appointment to visit guests, new attenders, absentees, and unchurched persons in the newcomers listing and/or city directory.

Confirm the appointment with a postcard, identifying the time and visitors.

Communicate the appointments to the person scheduling visitation.

Name and Address	Date/Time/ Type of Visit	Background Information

Worksheet 6

For use with Chapter 3

Survey Guide and Opinion Poll

The following attitudes and approaches seem to be effective in surveys.

Survey on Saturdays *after* 10:00 a.m. and in the evening (spring, summer, and fall) from 6:00 p.m. until dark.

Dress neatly and casually. Be modest and moderate.

Wear comfortable shoes!

Go by two's (for mutual encouragement).

Be courteous and consistently gracious. Smile!

Stay on the driveway and sidewalk (don't walk on the lawn).

Introduce yourself and state your purpose succinctly. "Hello! My name is *(name)*. I'm with one of the churches in the area, the *(name)* Church. I'm taking an opinion poll so that we can get to know the people in this area better. May I have your opinion?"

If persons do not want to respond, thank them and move on.

Thank "churched" respondents and move on. Be courteous, but do not get bogged down in conversation with believers. Our aim is to find unchurched persons.

Complete the opinion poll for each unchurched respondent. (See sample on p. 210.) Don't press; ask questions and respond to answers in a neutral manner. Ask for name, address, and phone. When a person is receptive, take time to talk. Jot down any pertinent information that is shared. Begin the process of becoming acquainted. Ask about their church background and experiences. Begin sharing about your church. Ask whether you may visit them in their home at another time. Suggest the next Wednesday evening around 8 o'clock as a possibility.

At the bottom of the opinion poll note your assessment of the degree of receptivity (to give guidance for further contacts).

Don't laugh or talk while walking away from the home.

Keep track of the streets you have surveyed.

Be persistent. Though most of the people will claim church involvement, resist thoughts of discouragement. Remember Psalm 126!

Worksheet 6 (Continued)

Opinion Poll

Hello! My name is _____. I'm with one of the churches in this area, the _____ Church. We're taking an opinion poll so that we can get to know the people in this area better. May we have your opinion on several quick questions?

1. Are you an active member of a nearby church?

   Yes   No

2. What do you think is the greatest need in (*name your city or area*)?

3. Why do you think most people don't attend church?

4. If you were looking for a church, what would you look for?

5. What advice can you give us? What could we do for you?

Thank you for your opinion! We appreciate your help. May we have your name, address, and phone so that we may keep in touch with you?

Notes:

Name _____

Address _____
                          Postal
City _____ Code _____

Phone _____

Worksheet 7

For use with Chapter 4

Personal Stories

In order to develop personal stories which you can share with persons as a witness, first think about the most satisfying benefits for you in your relationship with Christ, initially and subsequently. In the following list, check the three benefits which have been most satisfying to you.

Benefit	*rather than*	**Need**
assurance of eternal life		fear of death
forgiveness, peace		guilt, depression
purpose		purposelessness, drift, apathy
power		weakness, addiction
fellowship		loneliness
support in trouble		"solo" efforts
direction, new perspective		confusion, questions
love, better relationships		strife, jealousy, conflict
contentment		restlessness
security		anxiety, worries
self-control		self-indulgence, self-gratification
compassion		indifference
gentleness		harshness
confidence		fear of failure
optimism, faith		discouragement, despondency

_____   _____

_____   _____

_____   _____

Next, draw upon your memory to identify experiences, incidents, events, and situations which illustrate your *need* before you experienced these benefits. After you have done this, return to your memory bank to recall experiences, incidents, events, and situations in which you experienced the reality of this benefit in your life. Jot down words or phrases to describe the experience. With one or two others you may want to have an "I remember when . . ." session to jog your memory. In the mutual recalling and storytelling, you can help one another to remember significant events and milestones in your faith journey. Make some notes below, so you can remember them until the next meeting.

Your aim in this session is only to "stir up" stories and experiences from your own experience. In the next session you will shape them into a personal witness or testimony.

Notes:

Worksheet 8

For use with Chapter 5

Personal Testimony

Select one of the most meaningful benefits of receiving eternal life—as a theme for your testimony. (You may wish to refer to Worksheet 7.) Decide on two incidents or experiences which give a clear "picture" of your life before and after you received Christ. Write out a personal testimony—with a description and illustration of your life before and after you received Christ, and an explanation in between. (A sample testimony is on the next page.)

Before I received eternal life I . . .
(Illustration from personal experience)

Then I . . .
(The explanation for the change)

Since I received eternal life . . .
(Illustration from personal experience)

Worksheet 8 (Continued)

Sample Testimony

Before I received eternal life, I was afraid to die. I was not preoccupied with death—I didn't think about it much. But when circumstances of one kind or another forced me to think about death, I was afraid.

I remember one time I was driving on a beautiful interstate highway. There were trees and shrubs on both sides of the roadway and a broad grassy median in the center. I was sleepy—fighting to stay awake—and dozed off. I woke with a start when the car drifted into the loose stones on the shoulder of the road. A few miles later I dozed off a second time. This time, when I woke up, I was hurtling down the center median at 65 mph. Fortunately, there were no trees or bridges, just grass. By the time I slowed to a stop and then eased back onto the highway, I was wide awake. I realized how close I had come to death—and I was chilled by the thought of dying and not going to heaven.

Now that I have accepted Jesus Christ as my Savior and Lord, this fear has been replaced by peace.

Not long ago I was sitting at the dinner table with my family. My wife had served cornbread, and I got a piece caught in my throat. I tried to swallow it, and couldn't. I tried to cough it up, and couldn't. I kept trying one and then the other. But there was nothing I could do to dislodge it. I'm here now because Connie saw what was happening, ran around the table, and forced her fingers down my throat. It may not be the approved method, but it worked. We were a sober family for the rest of the meal. Once again, the prospect of death was front and center. But this time, I realized, I had not been afraid. I felt concern for my family, but no fear for myself. In its place, I have a deep settled peace because I know that when I die I will go to heaven.

Worksheet 9

For use with Chapter 6

Gospel Presentation
(An Expanded Outline)

(Adapted from the *Evangelism Explosion* presentation)

Note: Worksheet 10 is this same presentation, but with Bible study questions for use by the inquirer.

When we attempt to describe the difference that God makes in our lives, a number of words come to mind: "peace," "purpose," "power," "love," "joy," and more. Among them, there is one word which is often an accurate indicator of exactly where we stand (or perceive ourselves to stand) in relation to God. That word is "heaven."

Would you like to assess your relationship with God? These two questions will be helpful:

Have you come to the place in your spiritual life where you know for certain that if you were to die today, you would go to heaven?

Suppose you were to die today and stand before God and he were to say to you, "Why should I let you into my heaven?" What would you say?

Many people, even ones who have gone to church all their lives, are not really sure what will happen to them when they die. They *hope* to go to heaven. They are *striving* to go to heaven. But they do not really know *for sure*.

Often this uncertainty comes from a misunderstanding of what is involved in attaining eternal life and going to heaven. If we were to ask the average person what one must do to have eternal life, his or her answer would probably include one or more of the following: live a good life; obey the Ten Commandments;

follow the teachings and example of Jesus; love others; join a church and attend regularly.

All of these reflect the popular idea that eternal life in heaven is a reward to be won. But this widespread conception is a *mis*conception. The Bible announces the good news that . . .

I. Eternal life is a *gift*.

For the wages of sin is death, but the gift of God is eternal life in Christ Jesus our Lord (Rom. 6:23).

It is not earned or deserved.

For it is by grace you have been saved, through faith—and this not from yourselves, it is the gift of God—not by works, so that no one can boast (Eph. 2:8-9).

Eternal life, the greatest thing any of us could ever receive, is an unearned, undeserved *gift*. Once we understand what the Bible teaches about man, we see that it *has* to be a gift.

II. Man (humankind) is a sinner and cannot save himself.

The Bible teaches that every one of us in one way or another has failed to keep God's commandments—by our actions, by our words, and by our thoughts; both by the things we have done and the things we have left undone.

For all have sinned and fall short of the glory of God (Rom. 3:23).

The reason for this is that God's standard is so high.

Batting Average

Last summer we went to three local baseball games—and now we're "hooked" on our local farm team. We enjoy going to the games. And when players that we've gotten to know here are sent on to the major leagues, we take special pleasure in following the team statistics, to see how they are doing.

Some of them, because they are so new in the major leagues, are doing poorly—batting around .150. One or two have come on strong—with a batting average around .250. But none yet has matched the performance of a ballplayer like George Brett, who has batted around .350! That kind of batting average is the ultimate in the major leagues; all the players aspire to bat like that.

But what is a perfect batting average? What is the standard by which everyone is measured? 1.000! A poor batter averages .150. A good batter, .250. And an outstanding batter, .350. But no one ever manages a perfect average of 1.000. That is too far beyond the capacities of even our best athletes.

In a similar way, even the best of us fall short of "the glory of God."

Be perfect, therefore, as your heavenly Father is perfect (Matt. 5:48).

For whoever keeps the whole law and yet stumbles at just one point is guilty of breaking all of it (James 2:10).

F-86 Sabre Jet Fighter

Such high standards are not unusual, even in our human experience. I was reading excerpts from the book *Yeager*, an autobiography of test pilot Chuck Yeager. He told about the F-86 Sabre jet fighter which was being used by our armed forces around the world and on three or four occasions crashed for no apparent reason, killing the pilots. He was flying the F-86 once, doing a low roll about 150 feet from the ground, flying upside down, when one of the ailerons (a-le-ron) locked. He managed to get it working again, took the plane up to 15,000 feet and tried the same maneuver—with the same result. He landed and told his superior: "I know why these planes are crashing." They disassembled the jet's wings and discovered that a single bolt was installed upside down.

The F-86 Sabre jet was fatally flawed by the incorrect installation of a single bolt! In a similar way, even one sin disqualifies us from heaven.

(or use the next illustration)

Scrambled Eggs

Sometimes I cook breakfast so that Connie can sit with the girls as they practice piano. One of my better meals is scrambled eggs, though I usually manage to forget one thing or another. Suppose one morning one of the eggs is rotten and, not having enough experience to know what to look for, I mix the rotten egg in with the five good ones. I add the milk, butter, and, when it's almost finished, some cheese—so that it looks mouth-watering. But what response will I get? Yelling, and spitting . . . because one rotten egg will spoil the whole dish.

When we attempt to serve up our lives to God, we might have many things in them which we call good. Yet when they are also filled with actions and thoughts that are rotten, how can we expect them to be acceptable to God?

This predicament in which we find ourselves comes into sharper focus when we look at what the Bible tells us about God.

III. **God is loving—and does not want to punish us; but he is also just—and, therefore, must punish our sins.**
    God is love (1 John 4:8b).
    Yet he does not leave the guilty unpunished (Ex. 34:7b).

God solved this dilemma in the most amazing way—by entering the world himself in the person of Jesus Christ.

IV. **Jesus Christ . . .**
    Who he is:
    In the beginning was the Word, and the Word was with God, and the Word was God. . . . The Word became flesh and lived for a while among us. We have seen his glory, the glory of the one and only Son, who came from the Father, full of grace and truth (John 1:1,14).

What he did:

Record Book of Sin

Imagine that this book is a minutely detailed record of my sins; it includes every action, every word, every thought that has been in violation of God's standards. Actually, it would take an encyclopedia . . . but this (book, held in right hand) is the problem—my sin. God loves me (lift right hand, still holding book) but he hates my sin and must punish it. To solve this problem God sent his son into the world (lift empty left hand).

The Bible says (in Isaiah 53:6): *"We all like sheep have gone astray. Each of us has turned to his own way, and the Lord has laid on him"*(transfer the book in one distinct motion from your right hand to your left hand, and leave it there) *"the iniquity of us all."*

God has punished Jesus for all of *my* sin and guilt. The punishment that should have been mine, Jesus suffered on the cross.

Tetelestai

Jesus' last words on the cross, "It is finished!", are fascinating in the original Greek. The Greek word is *tetelestai* (pronounced "tet-*tell*-es-tie"), a commercial word which means "paid in full." Just before he died, Jesus said, "It is paid—paid in full!"

As the unique God/man, Jesus could do something that no one else could do. Jesus Christ died to pay for our sins and to purchase a place for us in heaven, which he offers as a gift.

V. This gift is received by faith.

For it is by grace you have been saved, through faith (Eph. 2:8).

"Faith" is a broad word; we use it to describe a number of different things. Some kinds of faith named in the Bible are:

A. Intellectual faith

You believe that there is one God. Good! Even the demons believe that—and shudder (James 2:19).

(The demons speaking) *"What do you want with us, Son of God?" they shouted. "Have you come here to torture us before the appointed time?"* (Matt. 8:29).

B. Temporal faith

And without faith it is impossible to please God, because anyone who comes to him must believe that he exists and that he rewards those who earnestly seek him (Heb. 11:6).

C. Saving faith

They replied, "Believe in the Lord Jesus, and you will be saved—you and your household" (Acts 16:31).

Saving faith includes the first two kinds of faith and goes beyond—to a deeper level of trust.

Chair

I may believe that this chair (point to chair) exists. I may trust this chair to support some of my possessions (place an item on the chair). But my trust is incomplete until I trust the chair to support me.

If this chair represents Jesus Christ, I may believe that he exists, that he lived and died and rose—intellectual faith. I may trust him for a financial problem (place wallet on chair) or safety on a trip (place key ring on chair)—temporal faith. But my faith is incomplete and insufficient until I trust him for everything: to forgive my past sins, to direct my present life, and to secure my eternal future (sit on chair).

Saving faith is an act of my entire interior being. It is an act of the *mind*—in which I accept the suffering, death, and resurrection of Jesus Christ as payment for my sins. It is an act of the *heart* (or affections)—in which I respond to the love and God and, in turn, desire to love God with all my heart and mind and soul and strength. And it is an act of the *will*—in which I renounce my sins and am willing to turn from them.

It is a change of direction, a reorientation of life, a complete transfer of trust for all of life—from myself to Jesus Christ.

Does this make sense to you?

Would you like to receive the gift of eternal life?

You receive eternal life by responding to this good news with saving faith in which you . . .

Believe

Yet to all who received him, to those who believed in his name, he gave the right to become children of God (John 1:12).

To receive eternal life, we must understand and believe this good news: Jesus Christ is the Son of God. He suffered and died to free us from our sins and he rose to give us eternal life.

Repent

From that time on Jesus began to preach, "Repent, for the kingdom of heaven is near" (Matt. 4:17).

Second, we must repent—that is, we must turn away from all wrongdoing and purpose to obey Christ in everything. It takes time to learn to live in God's way, but the first step is to determine that we will. Repentance is a complete change of mind and direction.

Receive

Here I am! I stand at the door and knock. If anyone hears my voice and opens the door, I will go in and eat with him, and he with me (Rev. 3:20).

Third, we must receive Christ as Savior and Lord, inviting him into our life in prayer—like this one:

Lord Jesus Christ, I acknowledge that I have gone my own way. I have sinned in thought, word and deed. I am sorry for my sins. I turn from them in repentance.

I believe that you died for me, bearing my sins in your own body. I thank you for your great love.

Now I open the door. Come in, Lord Jesus. Come in as my Savior, and cleanse me. Come in as my Lord, and take control of me. And I will serve you, in fellowship with other Christians, as you give me strength, all my life. Amen.

Note: Worksheet 10 is this same presentation (without the illustrations), but with Bible study questions for use by the inquirer.

Worksheet 10

For use with Chapter 6

Gospel Presentation
(A Bible Study)

INTRODUCTORY SESSION—
THE GIFT OF ETERNAL LIFE

When we attempt to describe the difference that God makes when we open our lives to him, a number of words come to mind: peace, purpose, power, love, joy . . . and more. Among them, there is one word which is often an accurate indicator of exactly where we stand (or perceive ourselves to stand) in relation to God. That word is "heaven."

Would you like to assess your relationship with God? These two questions might be helpful.

Have you come to the place in your spiritual life where you know for certain that if you were to die today, you would go to heaven?

Suppose you were to die today and stand before God and he were to say to you, "Why should I let you into my heaven?" What would you say?

Most of us know definitely whether we are working and whether we are married. Yet often we do not know whether we have eternal life. We do not know whether we are going to heaven.

This uncertainty comes from a misunderstanding of what is involved in attaining eternal life and going to heaven. If we were to ask the average person what one must do to have eternal life, his or her answer would probably include one or more of the following:

_____

_____

_____

_____

_____

All of these reflect the popular idea that eternal life in heaven is a reward to be won. But this widespread conception is a *mis*conception. The Bible teaches that . . .

I. Eternal life is a *gift*.

A. How is eternal life described in Romans 6:23? _____
_____

B. In Ephesians 2:8-9, what is the contrasting approach?

_____

_____

Eternal life, the greatest thing any of us could ever receive, is an unearned, undeserved *gift*. Once we understand what the Bible teaches about man, we see that it has to be a gift.

II. Man (humankind) is a sinner and cannot save himself.

A. The Bible teaches that every one of us in one way or another has failed to keep God's commandments—by our actions, by our words and by our thoughts; both by the things we have done and the things we have left undone. According to Romans 3:23, are there any exceptions? _____

B. According to Matthew 5:48 and James 2:10, why is this?
Matthew 5:48 _____

_____

James 2:10 _____

_____

C. Can you think of similar circumstances in our human experience? _____

This predicament in which we find ourselves comes into sharper focus when we look at what the Bible tells us about God.

III. God is loving—and does not want to punish us; but he is also just—and, therefore, must punish our sins.
   A. How does 1 John 4:8 describe God? _____
   B. But the same Bible also tells us what in Exodus 34:7?

   _____

   _____

God solved this dilemma in the most amazing way—by entering the world himself in the person of Jesus Christ.

IV. Jesus Christ . . .
   A. Who is he:
      John 1:1, 14 _____

   _____

   _____

   _____

   B. What he did:
      Isaiah 53:6 _____

   _____

   _____

As the unique God/man, Jesus Christ could do something that no one else could do. He died to pay for our sins and to purchase a place for us in heaven, which he offers as a gift.

V. This gift is received by faith.
   A. According to Ephesians 2:8, how may we receive the gift of eternal life? _____

   _____

   B. "Faith" is a broad word; we use it to describe a number of different things. What are some of the kinds of faith named in the Bible?
      James 2:19; Matthew 8:29 _____
      Hebrews 11:6 _____
      Acts 16:31 _____
   Saving faith includes the first two kinds of faith and goes beyond—to a deeper level of trust.
      Saving faith is an act of my entire interior being. It is an act of the *mind*—in which I accept the suffering, death, and resurrection of Jesus Christ as payment for my sins. It is an act of the *heart* (or affections)—in which I respond to the love of God and, in turn, desire to love God with all my heart and mind and soul and

strength. And it is an act of the *will*—in which I renounce my sins and am willing to turn from them.

It is a change of direction, a reorientation of life, a complete transfer of trust for all of life—from myself to Jesus Christ. Does this make sense to you? Would you like to receive the gift of eternal life? You receive eternal life by responding to this good news with saving faith in which you . . .

Believe

Yet to all who received him, to those who believed in his name, he gave the right to become children of God (John 1:12).

To receive eternal life, we must understand and believe this good news: Jesus Christ is the Son of God. He suffered and died to free us from our sins and he rose to give us eternal life.

Repent

From that time on Jesus began to preach, "Repent, for the kingdom of heaven is near" (Matt. 4:17).

Second, we must repent—that is, we must turn away from all wrongdoing and purpose to obey Christ in everything. It takes time to learn to live in God's way, but the first step is to determine that we will. Repentance is a complete change of mind and direction.

Receive

"Here I am! I stand at the door and knock. If anyone hears my voice and opens the door, I will come in and eat with him, and he with me" (Rev. 3:20).

Third, we must receive Christ as Savior and Lord, inviting him into our life in prayer—like this one:

Lord Jesus Christ, I acknowledge that I have gone my own way. I have sinned in thought, word and deed. I am sorry for my sins. I turn from them in repentance.

I believe that you died for me, bearing my sins in your own body. I thank you for your great love.

Now I open the door. Come in, Lord Jesus. Come in as my Savior, and cleanse me. Come in as my Lord, and take control of me. And I will serve you, in fellowship with other Christians, as you give me strength, all my life. Amen.

Worksheet 11

For use with Chapter 6

Good News

(Based on Paul Cedar's "Night of Caring")

Today's newspaper is filled with news, much of it bad news.

When Jesus began his public teaching, he announced good news! *"The time has come,"* he said. *"The kingdom of God is near. Repent and believe that good news"* (Mark 1:15).

With this announcement Jesus began to demonstrate what he meant by good news. He offered two men, Simon and Andrew, a new sense of *purpose* (Mark 1:17). To his listeners he gave the *widsom* of his teaching (Mark 1:22). Jesus responded to one man's plea with *healing* (Mark 1:40-42). To another man he granted *forgiveness* (Mark 2:10-12). To the "bad" people of the day, he offered *hope* (Mark 2:17). To everyone who followed him, he promised a life that was full and eternal (Mark 10:29-30).

Jesus announces the same good news to us. We may have a life that is full of purpose, wisdom, healing, forgiveness, and hope—and one that will last forever.

Sadly, many people are moving farther away from this kind of life.

We want to experience these things. Yet we insist on seeking them in our own way, rather than in God's way. The Bible describes our misdirection like this:

We all, like sheep, have gone astray, each of us has turned to his own way . . . (Isa. 53:6)

There is a way that seems right to a man, but in the end it leads to death (Prov. 14:12).

Sometimes our thoughts, words, and actions are flagrantly wrong. At other times we might justifiably consider ourselves as good as the next person. But the basic problem is essentially the same: we are choosing to go our own way rather than God's.

purpose
wisdom
healing
forgiveness
hope   ═══════════════⟹   S𝕀ℕ
eternal hope

The result of rejecting (or simply ignoring) God's way is ultimately hurtful to ourselves and others. We may experience financial difficulties, interpersonal crises, emotional stress, failing health, or a gnawing internal restlessness. Often we can identify attitudes and behaviors which are causing these difficulties, and we resolve to change.

Typically, our good intentions motivate us for several weeks or months . . . and then we fall back into our former patterns of living. The Bible describes this common experience:

> *I have the desire to do what is good, but I cannot carry it out. For what I do is not the good I want to do; no, the evil I do not want to do—this I keep on doing* (Rom. 7:18-19).

In our own strength we are doomed to continual disappointment—to a recurring cycle of good intentions and subsequent failures. The Bible expresses the frustration and defeat we often feel:

> *What a wretched man I am! Who will rescue me from this body of death?* (Rom. 7:24).

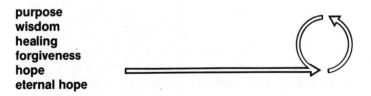

purpose
wisdom
healing
forgiveness
hope
eternal hope

In the next sentence the Bible answers this question:

Thanks be to God—through Jesus Christ our Lord!

The *good news* that Jesus announces is that he can break this frustrating pattern. Jesus—and only Jesus—can save us from this recurring cycle of determination and defeat.

Salvation is found in no one else, for there is no other name under heaven given to men by which we must be saved (Acts 4:12).

In his suffering and death on the cross, Jesus Christ has suffered the consequences of our willfulness—or our sin. He has taken the penalty upon himself and now, in its place, offers us the forgiveness and empowerment which enables us to turn away from sin and toward God.

We all, like sheep, have gone astray, each of us has turned to his own way; and the Lord has laid on him the inquity of us all (Isa. 53:6).

(Jesus) himself bore our sins in his body on the tree, so that we might die to sins and live for righteousness; by his wounds you have been healed (1 Pet. 2:24).

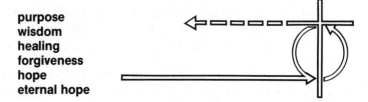

purpose
wisdom
healing
forgiveness
hope
eternal hope

Jesus himself tells us how we can receive this forgiveness and empowerment.

"If anyone would come after me, he must deny himself and take up his cross and follow me" (Mark 8:34).

The first step is to *deny ourself.*

This phrase means, literally, to say "no" to ourselves—that is, to all the thoughts, words, and actions that we know to be wrong. We must decisively turn away from all sin. We may have attempted this same change of direction before. But this time we will have Jesus' help.

purpose
wisdom
healing
forgiveness
hope
eternal hope

The second step is to *take up our cross.*

At other places the Bible emphasizes the need to *believe* that Jesus died for us, bearing our sins in his own body, and to *receive* him into our lives in a conscious personal decision.

Yet to all who received him, to those who believed in his name, he gave the right to become children of God (John 1:12).

"Here I am! I stand at the door and knock. If anyone hears my voice and opens the door, I will come in and eat with him, and he with me" (Rev. 3:20).

In the phrase "take up our cross" Jesus stresses absolute commitment. When we believe in Jesus and receive him into our lives, we commit ourselves to follow him anywhere, even to death.

In this phrase Jesus pictured a scene that was common in Palestine at the time—a condemned prisoner on his way to execution, carrying the cross on which he would die. His point: you must be willing to believe in and obey me unconditionally, even to the point of death.

You can make an unconditional commitment to Jesus with a prayer like this:

Lord Jesus Christ, I acknowledge that I have gone my own way. I have sinned in thought, word, and deed. I am sorry for my sins. I turn from them in repentance.

I believe that you died for me, bearing my sins in your own body. I thank you for your great love.

Now I open the door. Come in, Lord Jesus. Come in as my Savior, and cleanse me. Come in as my Lord, and take control of me. And I will serve you, in fellowship with other Christians, as you give me strength, all of my life. Amen.

purpose
wisdom
healing
forgiveness
hope
eternal hope

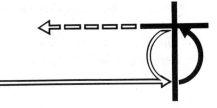

The third step is to *follow* Jesus.

To follow Jesus is to walk in the same direction, following his example, progressing toward his character, and doing his work in his forgiveness and power. Jesus does not demand perfection. His concern is with our direction. When we follow Jesus, we are progressing in his character and work, one step at a time.

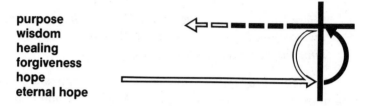

**purpose
wisdom
healing
forgiveness
hope
eternal hope**

Immediately after Jesus explains how we can surrender our lives to him, he describes the result we can anticipate:

> *"For whoever wants to save his life will lose it, but whoever loses his life for me and for the gospel will save it"* (Mark 8:35).

A decision to change direction by renouncing our sinful desires, making an absolute commitment to Jesus, and following him in obedience can be a frightening one, because we are turning away from convictions and practices by which we have conducted our life. In a real sense, we are losing the life we have known up to this point.

But Jesus has promised—when we lose our life in this way, we will save it. Our desires for a life of purpose, wisdom, healing, forgiveness, and hope will be fulfilled—yes, beyond our expectations. And we will live forever.

Are you ready now to act on this good news?

"The time has come," Jesus said. *"The kingdom of God is near. Repent and believe the good news."*

Worksheet 12

For use with Chapter 9

Home Visits

Objectives

1. Get acquainted

How long have you lived here?

Where did you live before?

How did you happen to move here?

How do you like it here?

How many children do you have?

What sort of work do you do?

How did you happen to pick this line of work?

2. Find out about church experience (team leader)

Were you involved with church in (name their previous home)?

What kind of church experiences have you had?

(Name of the appointment caller) said you were looking for a church home.

What kind of church are you looking for?

3. Share a church testimony and personal testimony (team members)

The thing I appreciate most about our church is . . . (tell a story).

Best of all, most of the people in our church have an active, personal relationship with Jesus Christ and are experiencing his presence and help in their lives. In my own life . . . (tell stories!)

4. Invite them to church (and leave brochures)

5. Ask permission to pray

(continued on next page)

Home Visits
Do's and Don'ts

Do's	*Don'ts*
—Dress neatly and appropriately	—Park in driveway
—Arrive on time	—Walk across the grass
—Greet the family warmly	—Stand too close to the door (about three steps back is good)
—Be courteous	
—Be observant	—Ring the doorbell more than twice
—Be complimentary	—Talk down to people
—Be enthusiastic	—Exaggerate or lie
—Try to get all the family together	—Monopolize the conversation
—Include all the family in the conversation (especially the children)	—Interrupt when others are speaking
	—Pry into family affairs
—Be a good listener	—Ignore anyone
—Be accepting	—Be critical of our church (or any church) or join in family criticism
—Keep purpose clearly in mind	
—Offer advice carefully (and sparingly)	—Argue with the family
	—Pressure the family
—Keep visit within agreed upon time	—Stay too long
—Express joy of visit as you leave	—Talk (or laugh) as you are walking away from the home

Worksheet 13

For use with Chapter 9

Visitation Report

Date _____

Visit at the scheduled time with your purpose clearly in mind.
Immediately after you visit, *record* additional background
information; *write* and *mail* a postcard; *decide* on the most
effective follow-up (phone calls, letters, subsequent visits,
etc.) and *make assignments.*
Report to the evangelism team coordinator and, the following
week, to the entire team.
Review your follow-up for each person/family each week.

Name/Address/Phone	Background Information	Continuing Follow-up

Worksheet 14

For use with Chapter 9

Evangelistic Assignments

Semester _____

Prayer _____

_____

_____

_____

_____

Appointments _____

_____

_____

Testimony/Invitation Visits _____

_____

_____

Encouragement/Gospel _____
Presentation Visits
_____

_____

Teaching or _____
Special Projects
_____

Typing/Clerical _____

_____

_____

Childcare _____

_____

_____

Worksheet 15

For use with Chapter 9

Team Leader Job Description

Weekly
1. Greet worshippers (or arrange for greeters from the evangelism team).
2. Arrange for someone to take attendance (worship, Sunday school, the evangelism team) and record totals.
3. Be sure we have enough appointments/assignments for the evangelism team.
4. Lead evangelism team gatherings each week; direct (or delegate) music, prayer, reporting/encouragement, Bible study, and assignments.
5. Keep a record of evangelism statistics.

Monthly
6. Make assignments in consultation with the pastor.
   Review prospects (invitation, encouragement, gospel presentation, teaching).
   Develop projects (special events, journalism, etc.).
   Designate team leaders.
   Assign teams.
7. Oversee maintainance of a current mailing list of evangelistic prospects (with addresses, phone numbers, and background notations).
8. Attend the meetings of the congregation's governing board and articulate outreach/evangelism concerns.

Periodically
9. Prepare a four/five month review of evangelism team activities.
10. Plan an appreciation dinner at the end of May.
11. Write a recruitment letter; ask the pastor to preach a recruitment message; and plan for "kickoff" dinner in September.
12. Attend a seminar or conference on evangelism and/or church growth each year (as church finances permit).

Worksheet 16

For use with Chapter 13

Sample of Evangelistic Team Profile

"RESCUE"

AIM: To mobilize the men/women/youth of our congregation in the work of evangelism—in a midweek "gathering/scattering" packed with inspiration, motivation, teaching, training and opportunity!

NAME: R Reaching,
E Equipping,
S Sending:
C Calling
U the Unchurched
E to Eternal Life!

TIME: Wednesday, from 7:00 to 9:00 p.m.

TASKS: A number of tasks are crucial to our total effort, such as:

Prayer—Our first and most basic task is prayer. When our pray-ers focus their prayers on evangelism each Wednesday evening, great things happen!

Encouragement—We give encouragement and support to persons who attend our church. With short, friendly telephone conversations, we can express concern and support. In times of illness or special need, we visit in homes and hospitals.

Telephoning—One way to find persons who may be interested in our church is by telephone. Each week we contact newcomers in our area to discover whether we can serve their need for a church home.

Visitation—We visit new persons (by appointment) to become acquainted and to introduce ourselves and our church. We share our testimonies and, when it is helpful, present the basic gospel message.

Teaching—As persons come to Christ and the church, we provide teaching on basic Christian maturity one-to-one in their homes.

Childcare—Some persons are eager to work in RESCUE, but need good care for their children in order to participate. We provide care at our meeting place and, at times, in individual homes.

Typing—This work "behind the scenes" enables us to maintain lists of current and prospective participants, prepare materials, and send letters.

Journalism—Our RESCUE team uses a variety of printed materials—a newsletter, brochures, booklets, handouts, and printed testimonies. To develop and produce these attractive pieces we need persons with writing, editing, layout, and printing/photocopying skills.

Statistics—We regularly measure our church's "vital signs." When these statistics are recorded and graphed, we have a clear picture of our congregation's health and development.

GOAL: Total mobilization of our membership for RESCUE!

Notes

[1] C. Peter Wagner, quoted by Devon Bontrager, "Evangelism, Pacifism, and Optimism," *Shalom*, Fall 1985, p. 3.

[2] Conversation with Oklahoma wheat farmers, J. Eugene Blackketter and Vernon Frymire, based on 1987 statistics compiled by the Oklahoma State University Agricultural Extension Service.

[3] Robert Schuller, quoted in C. Wayne Zunkle, *Growing the Small Church*, (Elgin, Ill.: David C. Cook Publishing Company, 1982), p. 31.

[4] C. Peter Wagner, Course Notebook *Church Growth I*, Fuller Theological Seminary (Extension class in Oklahoma City: June 11-22, 1984), in the section titled "Biblical Principles for Strategies for Growth," pp. 4-5.

[5] Rebecca Manley Pippert, *Out of the Salt-shaker and into the World* (Downers Grove, Ill.: InterVarsity Press, 1979), p. 100.

[6] Samuel Shoemaker, quoted in Joyce Nevelle, *How to Share Your Faith Without Being Offensive* (New York: The Seabury Press, 1983), p. 5.

[7] Rosalind Rinker, quoted in Joyce Nevelle, *op. cit.*, p. 4.

[8] The clearest and most helpful introduction to the subject, in my estimation, has been in *Power Evangelism*, written by John Wimber in collaboration with Kevin Springer (San Francisco: Harper & Row, 1986). This readable and comprehensive explanation of the place of signs and wonders in evangelism is helpful for skeptics and enthusiasts alike. The book shows that evangelism, with signs and wonders, can be compatible with conservative evangelical perspective and practice. As. C. Peter Wagner observes in the preface, "In this book John Wimber provides clues to a powerful spiritual instrument which, when used with dedication and discernment, could advance the process of world evangelism by a quantum leap."

[9] John Wimber, *Power Evangelism* (San Francisco: Harper & Row, 1986), p. 113f.

[10] Steve Clark, *Growing in Faith* (Ann Arbor, Mich.: Servant Books, 1972), p. 28f.

[11] D. James Kennedy, *Evangelism Explosion*, revised edition (Wheaton, Ill.: Tyndale House Publishers, 1970), p. 26ff.

[12] Oswald Hoffman, "Turn the Gospel Loose," *Leadership Magazine*, Fall 1985, p. 14.

[13] Paul Cedar, in his training course entitled "Night of Caring" (Pasadena, Calif.: Dynacom Ministries, 1982).

[14] Bill Bright, "Four Spiritual Laws" (Arrowhead Springs, Calif.: Campus Crusade for Christ, Inc., 1965).

[15] Jointly published by Youth for Christ/ USA (Wheaton, Ill.) and Campus Crusade for Christ International (San Bernardino, Calif.), 1985.

[16] Joseph C. Aldrich, *Life-Style Evangelism* (Portland, Ore.: Multnomah Press, 1978), pp. 221-223.

[17] Noted in John Zercher, *Lantern in the Dawn* (Nappanee, Ind.: Evangel Press, 1980), p. 130.

[18] Pippert, *op. cit.*, p. 141.

[19]InterVarsity Christian Fellowship, cited in Pippert, *op. cit.*, p. 179.

[20]Kennedy, *op. cit.*, pp. 24-44.

[21]Quoted by Pippert, *op. cit.*, p. 96.

[22]John R. W. Stott, *Basic Christianity*, Second Edition (Grand Rapids, Mich., William B. Eerdmans Publishing Co., 1986), p. 129.

[23]Jim Berlucchi, *Person to Person* (Ann Arbor, Mich.: Servant Books, 1984), p. 100f.

[24]*Ibid.*.

[25]Charles Colson, *Who Speaks for God?* (Westchester, Ill.: Crossway Books, 1985), p. 95.

[26]*Basic Christian Maturity* (Ann Arbor, Mich.: Word of Life, 1975), p. 71f.

[27]Information about these courses can be obtained at the following addresses: *Evangelism Explosion International*, P.O. Box 23820, Fort Lauderdale, FL 33307; *GRADE Ministry*, Box 2000, Marion, IN 46952; *Dynacom Communications*, 393 North Lake Ave., Pasadena, CA 91101.

[28]Robert Coleman, *The Master Plan of Evangelism*, (Old Tappen, N.J.: Spire Books, a division of Fleming H. Revell Company, 1963).

[29]Peter S. Williamson, "What Did It Mean To Be a Disciple?" *Pastoral Renewal*, July 1978, pp. 1-5.

[30]Paul Anderson, "A Pat on the Back or a Kick in the Pants?" *Pastoral Renewal*, September 1984, pp. 22, 30.

[31]Win Arn, "Can We Close the Back Door?" *Pastoral Renewal*, February 1986, p. 119.

[32]Bruce Manning Metzger, *The New Testamant: Its Background, Growth, and Development* (Nashville, Tenn.: Abingdon Press, 1965), pp. 79-96.

[33]*Ibid.*, p. 216.

[34]Bob Waymire and Peter Wagner, *The Church Growth Survey Handbook* (Global Church Growth Bulletin, P. O. Box 66, Santa Clara, Calif.)

[35]Pippert, *op. cit.*, p. 167.

[36]Grace Holland, "Who Are the Nations?" *Evangelical Visitor*, December 1986, pp. 13-14.

[37]*Ibid.*, p. 14.

[38]Stephen Sorenson, director of communications for International Students Incorporated (ISI), quoted by Kevin Springer, "The World at Your Doorstep," *Equipping the Saints*, September/October 1987, p. 5.

[39]Frank R. Tillipaugh, *Unleashing the Church* (Ventura, Calif.: Regal Books, a division of GL Publications, 1982), p. 189.

[40]*Ibid.*, p. 16.

[41]"A Case in Point," *World Evangelization*, March, 1987, p. 16.